"Getting the gospel right is an absolut
how the gospel applies to every dimension of the ... and joys for every believer. Mitch Chase brings great wisdom and clarity for this challenge in *The Gospel Is for Christians*. Read it for the sound counsel and good news you will find here."

—Dr. R. Albert Mohler Jr.
President, The Southern Baptist Theological Seminary

"The gospel is not just for unbelievers. The gospel is not just a kind of good news key that allows people to unlock the doors to heaven. The gospel is life. The gospel saves, and it sustains. Mitch Chase loves this gospel, and in this book, he faithfully proclaims it. Written in an engaging, winsome way, this book will challenge and shape you. It will tell you why you need to believe the gospel to have eternal life and why you need to dwell upon this gospel, love it, feed upon it, and depend upon it every day. The gospel is for Christians and so, too, is this book. I highly recommend it to you."

—Tim Challies
Author of *The Discipline of Spiritual Discernment*
and *The Next Story: Faith, Friends, Family, and the Digital World*

"In *The Gospel Is for Christians*, Mitch Chase demonstrates not merely a love for theology but a love for the Savior to whom all good theology points. Mitch reminds us that the good news of Jesus Christ is not a peripheral matter for the Christian. The gospel must remain at the center of our spiritual life in order to bear the fruits of ongoing repentance and faith."

—Dr. Trevin Wax
Author of *This Is Our Time: Everyday Myths in Light of the Gospel*
and *Eschatological Discipleship: Leading Christians to Understand Their Historical and Cultural Context*

"The gospel is needed not just for the starting line of the Christian life but the finish line. It is how you enter, endure, and ultimately reach the end of the journey as a follower of Jesus. Mitch Chase has done the church a great service by writing this book. Read it slowly, meditate on it bit by bit, and be encouraged as you consider how you need the gospel just as much as your lost friends and neighbors do."

—Dr. Andrew Hébert
Lead Pastor of Paramount Baptist Church, Amarillo, Texas

"In a crowded field of gospel-centered books and studies, Mitchell Chase has written a helpful and unique contribution that takes our eyes off ourselves and onto the God who has saved us. May this book help many remember that the gospel matters every day, all the time, for everyone."

—Dr. Brandon D. Smith
Assistant Professor of Theology and New Testament, Cedarville University
Author of *Rooted: Theology for Growing Christians*
and *They Spoke of Me: How Jesus Unlocks the Old Testament*

"In a context that often minimizes the gospel as something only to be shared with unbelievers or that trivializes the gospel by turning it into an all-purpose adjective, Chase brings needed clarity to what the gospel is and how the good news of Jesus impacts the entirety of the Christian life."

—Dr. Dustin Bruce
Dean of Boyce College, Louisville, Kentucky

THE
GOSPEL
IS FOR
CHRISTIANS
SECOND EDITION

MITCHELL L. CHASE

LUCIDBOOKS

For Stacie, my beloved wife and precious gift from God,
who loves the gospel and lives in its light

TABLE OF CONTENTS

PREFACE

Jesus says the way to life—to *real* life, the kind only a Creator could grant—is a narrow path (Matt. 7:13–14). Imagine you're in a car traveling on this path. You've left your starting place. You can see it in the rearview mirror fading into the background, looking more distant every moment. Soon you can't see it in the mirror at all. You're just moving onward, eyes ahead, anticipating your destination. But the starting place that you left wasn't the gospel. The gospel is the car you're in. The gospel isn't a thing we leave behind after salvation. The narrow path is a gospel journey.

There's a subtle danger to familiar ideas because being familiar with something doesn't mean understanding it. And *gospel* is one of those words that makes its way around Christian circles in all sorts of expressions. "Have you heard the gospel?" "I believe the gospel." "Live out the gospel." "Preach the gospel." "Are you gospel-centered?" "I love the gospel." "Defend the gospel."

You get the point. During most of my years as a Christian, I thought of the gospel as what unbelievers needed. And most certainly they do need it. The gospel announces a Savior for sinners, and his name is Jesus. He is a redeeming King.

But the book you're holding is my plea for you to follow Christ with a gospel-loving heart. If the gospel is important for the unsaved, is it now unimportant for the saved? By no means (to quote a man from Tarsus)! The disciple of Jesus needs the gospel of Jesus. And if you'll walk with me through the next 10 chapters, I'll show you what I mean.

1
CHRIST THE CENTER

Before there was a world, there was a plan. God in his infinite wisdom wrote the story of the ages, and the sum and center of that story is Jesus Christ. The story of Jesus is the gospel—the *good news*. And this news is not *about* you but *for* you. God's story ordained a Sunday morning when some women went to a tomb, only to find it empty because the occupant had risen from the dead. And because that happened, we need to ask some questions. Why did he rise? Why did he die? Was his death a tragedy, the result of a popular teacher clashing with the Roman Empire? What if his death had been the plan all along? And what do the death and resurrection of Jesus mean for us?

For the Glory of God

We are not the center of the world. It is freeing to realize that the world doesn't revolve around us because we are then more equipped to live out our created purpose. As the Westminster Catechism says, the chief end of man is to glorify God and enjoy him forever. If we are going to glorify God, we will seek to honor the Son whom God has honored. Jesus has the name above every name, and at the name of Jesus every knee should bow to the glory of God the Father (Phil. 2:10–11).

When you read through the Bible, you get the sense that God prizes his glory. He created people for his glory (Isa. 43:7), and he doesn't share his glory with idols (Isa. 42:8). When God saves sinners, it's so he might display, in the coming ages, "the immeasurable riches of his grace in kindness toward us in Christ Jesus" (Eph. 2:7). His plan of redemption is "to the praise of his glorious grace" (Eph. 1:6). Even his judgment exalts his name and power (Exod. 9:16; Rom. 9:17).

Are you troubled by God's goal of doing all things for his glory? Maybe you wonder how that goal squares with his love for creation and his care for image-bearers in particular. But God's love for his glory does not cancel his love for us. God, who is of infinite worth, should be exalted, and if God exalted anything above himself, he would be an idolater.

When I first encountered the notion of God's God-centeredness, it reminded me of people who are overly into themselves. They can be off-putting, as if the sun rises because they wake up. If self-exaltation is wrong for us, why is God-exaltation right for God? Why is it right for God to be concerned about his name and glory in the world?

C. S. Lewis admitted that he struggled with the Bible's language about worshiping God. But Lewis realized that praise is what we do with things we love and enjoy. We sound the praises of art and people, of landscapes and food. Lewis said, "I think we delight to praise what we enjoy because the praise not merely expresses but completes the enjoyment; it is its appointed consummation."[1]

Praising God is the fitting expression of knowing and enjoying God. Since we were created to know the living God, the believer comes to see that exalting God is satisfying to the human heart. The exaltation of God is the highest moral act human beings can perform. The Bible is not shy about summoning people to worship. Just read the book of Psalms, which contains many calls to worship him. We should ascribe glory to God (Ps. 29:1–2), it is fitting to praise the Lord (Ps. 33:1), we should invite others to exalt the Lord with us (Ps. 34:3), all the nations of the world should shout to God with cries of praise (Ps. 47:1; 66:1–2), and praise belongs to God's name forever (Ps. 72:19).

We will not worship God rightly if we think he's overly concerned about his name and glory. If God thinks too much of himself, my praise of

---

1. C. S. Lewis, *Reflections on the Psalms* (New York: Harcourt Brace, 1958), 95.

him will be stunted rather than stimulated. But if it is right for God to call people to exalt his name and thus wrong for people to seek that glory for themselves, then my worship should not be hindered but invigorated by his greatness and worth.

Worth—that's the core issue. That's why God, and not man, should be praised. That's why God's name, and not man's, should be exalted. God is worthy of praise; we are not. Throughout the Psalms—and the Bible as a whole—God is the only one worthy of worldwide worship and glory. As a holy and righteous God, "a great God, and a great King above all gods" (Ps. 95:3), he should be praised. These realities don't imply that humans are worthless, but they are certainly not worthy of worship. In Isaiah, God asks all of us, "To whom then will you compare me, that I should be like him?" (Isa. 40:25). There is no worthy competitor of the glory due to God. He does what he does for his glory, and that is good. If God didn't pursue his glory in all things, he would not be worthy of worship. He's calling us to exalt the object of greatest worth—God.

Christ and All Things

As we think about God doing all things for his glory, we have to think about Jesus Christ, for God is bringing glory to his name in Christ. Paul says of Jesus, "For by him all things were created, in heaven and on earth, visible and invisible, whether thrones or dominions or rulers or authorities—all things were created through him and for him" (Col. 1:16). Who can plumb the depth of this verse? Paul has stated one of the most profound truths that can be uttered. Christ was before all things, "and in him all things hold together" (Col. 1:17).

Jesus is the *origin* of creation and the *sustainer* of creation. Natural laws aren't holding the universe together; Jesus is. Spontaneous and random interactions of atoms were not the agents of how things came to exist; Jesus was. God did not set the world in motion and then assume a passive stance to let the chips fall where they may. The Bible doesn't promote a deistic view of God. Rather, God made the world and sustains its existence through his Son. Jesus is the one "whom he appointed the heir of all things, through whom also he created the world" (Heb. 1:2).

Jesus is also the purpose of creation; all things were created *for* him (Col. 1:16). Creation exists for Jesus Christ. What we are seeing is that God's plan for all things is about his glory and name, but it is also about his glory and name being revealed in Jesus Christ his Son. Redemption has everything to do with Jesus. Christians were chosen in Christ before the foundation of the world (Eph. 1:4). Our adoption as God's children has been "through Jesus Christ" (Eph. 1:5). We were redeemed "through his blood" (Eph. 1:7). And God's plan for the fullness of time is "to unite all things"—everything in heaven and earth—in Christ (Eph. 1:10).

Christ and All Authority

If God desires to sum up all things in Christ and to do so for his glory, then he needs the authority to make that happen. If you want to make sweeping changes at your place of employment but don't have the badge or jurisdiction to do so, your plans are merely in your head. Without the necessary authority and influence, you cannot accomplish what someone could in a position higher than yours.

The good news is that God occupies the highest place. God is not head over some things or most things but *all* things. The New Testament sheds further light on the authority of God when it speaks of the supremacy and authority of Christ over all things. At the end of the Gospel of Matthew, Jesus gives the Great Commission to his disciples (Matt. 28:19–20). The preceding verse grounds the commission in the authority of Christ. Jesus tells his disciples, "All authority in heaven and on earth has been given to me" (Matt. 28:18).

Jesus is *Lord*—the Sovereign Master. You and I don't make him Lord; he has that role already. In Peter's address to a crowd gathered at Jerusalem during Pentecost, he told them that "God has made him both Lord and Christ, this Jesus whom you crucified" (Acts 2:36). Jesus is Lord and Christ because God raised Jesus from the dead (Acts 2:31–32), and he ascended to the right hand of God (Acts 2:33–35). As the risen and ascended Son of God, Jesus is supreme. The word *Lord* denotes sovereign rule, and that is precisely what Jesus has. Paul wrote about the total authority of Jesus. He said Jesus reigns "far above all rule and authority and power and dominion, and above every name that is named, not only in this age but also in the one to come" (Eph. 1:21).

When sinners believe in Jesus as their Savior, Jesus is already Lord before their confession. Sinners who believe in Jesus are acknowledging his lordship, but Jesus is Lord whether or not they believe in him. We cannot *make* Jesus anything, much less Lord. The lordship of Jesus over unbelievers means they are accountable. They are bound for judgment if they do not repent and live by faith in him under his lordship. Unbelievers should believe in Jesus because he *is* Lord.

A Lamb to Be Slain

Jesus is Lord of all things because of what he did in his work as our Lamb. In the last book of the Bible, the apostle John tells of a Lamb who was slain (Rev. 13:8). The New Testament teaches that Jesus is this Lamb of God. When another John—this time the Baptist, not the apostle—saw Jesus, he declared, "Behold, the Lamb of God, who takes away the sin of the world!" (John 1:29).

In the system of Israel's offerings in the Old Testament, a lamb was an example of a flock sacrifice. Right before the divine deliverance of Israel from captivity in Egypt, the Israelites sacrificed lambs and smeared blood on their doorposts (Exod. 12:21–28). The lamb was a substitute. Judgment fell on the sacrifice so the offerer could be pardoned.

Jesus was the slain Lamb of God, the sacrifice we needed, yet we were completely undeserving. His slaying was crucifixion. The book of Revelation bears out the significance of this sacrifice: Jesus "loves us and has freed us from our sins by his blood" (Rev. 1:5). In his death, Jesus "ransomed people for God from every tribe and language and people and nation" (Rev. 5:9).

A Promise before the Ages

The ransom of people for God was to secure the "hope of eternal life" (Titus 1:2). God promised this hope "before the ages began," and in the fullness of time, he sent his Son to accomplish the mission of redemption (Titus 1:2–3). The good news of Jesus Christ was prepared before creation. The cross was not Plan B.

Using language of divine necessity, Jesus himself taught that he *must* be rejected and killed (Mark 8:31; cf. 10:33–34). He spoke of his death as fulfilling scripture (Luke 18:31–33). And since God doesn't leave his promises unfulfilled, Jesus's death was as sure as God was trustworthy. God had promised the hope of eternal life, and he never lies (Titus 1:2). Jesus didn't die against the will of God. On the contrary, Isaiah said that it was the will of Yahweh to crush the suffering Servant (Isa. 53:10).

With these scriptures in view, we can ask and answer two important questions. First, who ultimately planned the murder of Jesus? God did. Second, when did God plan the death of his Son? He planned it before he made the world.

If God always planned to send his Son into the world, then the cross was not a necessary adjustment that God made after Adam and Eve sinned. John Piper's words are helpful here: "The biblical view is that the sufferings and death of Christ for sin are not planned after the actual sin of Adam but before. Therefore, when the sin of Adam happens, God is not surprised by it, but has already made it part of his plan."[2] God created the world knowing that Adam and Eve would sin. Since no one forced God to create, and since God exercised his will in creating, it is appropriate to say that God incorporated the disobedience of Adam and Eve into his plan.

The Disciples before the Cross

The people in Jesus's earthly ministry didn't embrace the cross as God's plan for the Messiah. In fact, the disciples initially rejected what Jesus taught

---

2. John Piper, *Spectacular Sins: And Their Global Purpose in the Glory of Christ* (Wheaton, IL: Crossway Books, 2008), 59.

them about his impending death. Does this surprise you? We might expect the disciples to fully support the details of Jesus's earthly mission. But the expectation of death bothered them.

On one occasion, when Jesus was teaching the disciples about his necessary suffering and death, Peter took him aside and began to rebuke him (Mark 8:31–32). In Matthew's account, Peter told Jesus, "Far be it from you, Lord! This shall never happen to you" (Matt. 16:22). Representing the other disciples, Peter's views corresponded to the prevailing idea about the Jewish Messiah, that the Anointed One (what Messiah or Christ means) would come to overthrow the political powers oppressing Jerusalem, not die on a cross. Peter meant well with his words. Perhaps he was correcting a misinformed Jesus. Didn't Jesus know that a crucified Messiah was an oxymoron?

Because the Jews expected political triumph and royal pomp, Jesus avoided the reinforcement of such messianic misunderstanding. When they thirsted for kingly showmanship and signs of political upheaval, Jesus modeled humility and gentleness instead. On the Sunday before Jesus was crucified, he rode into Jerusalem on a donkey (John 12:12, 14). The Jerusalem crowd waved palm branches (a symbol of national deliverance) in anticipation of Jesus subverting their political oppressors and setting up his throne. But he appeared on a donkey, not a war horse. John wrote, "His disciples did not understand these things at first" (John 12:16). The crowd was confused, as well as the disciples. If Jesus was the Messiah, did he know what he was doing?

Fast-forward to Jesus's arrest. When armed men seized Jesus, "they all left him and fled" (Mark 14:50). The disciples did not stay with Jesus. Their self-preservation instincts prevailed, especially since Jesus's predictions of suffering were materializing. Peter had earlier insisted to Jesus, "If I must die with you, I will not deny you," and all the other disciples said the same (Mark 14:31). But despite their insistence of loyalty, the disciples deserted Jesus at his arrest, and Peter explicitly denied knowing him three times (Mark 14:30, 66–72).

The desertion by Jesus's followers was all part of God's plan. In Mark 14:27, Jesus quoted Zechariah 13:7 as scriptural proof that his disciples would desert him: "I will strike the shepherd, and the sheep will be scattered." The shepherd (Jesus) was struck during the events of his suffering, which commenced with his arrest, and the sheep (the disciples) fled. All scripture pointing to Jesus's suffering would be fulfilled, no matter how tragic the fulfillment would seem.

A Dead Messiah

We shouldn't be hard on the disciples. Jewish leaders labeled any messianic claimants who died as messianic pretenders. A dead messiah was a false messiah. For the Jewish leaders, Jesus's death was a victory on their part; they executed a problematic teacher who was leading people astray with his blasphemous claims and actions. The thorn in their side was gone.

For the disciples, however, Jesus's death was a colossal embarrassment. When Jesus appeared to his disciples after his resurrection, they had locked themselves in a home because of their fear of the Jews (John 20:19). The events of Jesus's suffering and death had provoked disillusionment and humiliation. Rather than announcing Jesus's triumph over sin, they hid in the face of his apparent defeat.

It is understandable that the disciples would flee and hide in despair. Those men had left everything to follow Jesus for the years of his earthly ministry. Now, the one on whom they had banked their hopes was arrested, led away, and killed. Even though Jesus explicitly predicted he would endure such treatment, his disciples were disenchanted as the events unfolded. When the guards ushered Jesus away, the disciples must have felt like their whole world was falling apart.

The Disciples after the Resurrection

The disciples' despair was only temporary. Jesus had told them, "Truly, truly, I say to you, you will weep and lament, but the world will rejoice. You will be sorrowful, but your sorrow will turn into joy" (John 16:20). The sinful world rejoiced at the death of Jesus while the disciples were mourning in anguish. But when the disciples encountered the risen Lord, their grief turned into joy (John 20:20).

The disciples were not the same people after they encountered the risen Jesus. The pre-resurrection disciples seemed timid and fearful, hiding with embarrassment and hopelessness. But the post-resurrection disciples were bold, courageous, and faithful. Before they encountered the risen Jesus, they never imagined that most of them would eventually give their lives for the sake of the Lord's commission (Matt. 28:18–20).

In the book of Acts, the very same disciples who once thought the idea of Jesus's resurrection seemed absurd began to proclaim in Jerusalem that God had raised Jesus from the dead. While Jews believed there would be a bodily resurrection at the end of history (Dan. 12:2; John 5:29), these disciples began spreading the message that God had, *in the middle of human history*, performed a bodily resurrection, and that the one raised was none other than Jesus of Nazareth. This message—part of what makes the gospel such good news—didn't exclude end-time hopes and promises, but it did show that God wasn't leaving all his reconciling, restoring, and transforming work for the very end of human history. God was beginning new creation now, inaugurating it in the resurrection of Jesus.

Peter, who once rebuked Jesus (Mark 8:31–32), had a different perspective on the cross after he encountered the risen Lord. In Jerusalem, Peter said to a crowd:

> *Men of Israel, hear these words: Jesus of Nazareth, a man attested to you by God with mighty works and wonders and signs that God did through him in your midst, as you yourselves know—this Jesus, delivered up according to the definite plan and foreknowledge of God, you crucified and killed by the hands of lawless men.*
>
> —Acts 2:22–23

Peter's understanding is not just a nuanced version of his previous view. There is a massive shift in perspective. Peter now describes Jesus's suffering as God's "definite plan." God had purposed the death of his Son, and that's why Jesus suffered under the hands of wicked men. Before the resurrection, Peter thought Jesus's death was an embarrassing disqualification from his role as God's Anointed One, but now Peter saw the cross as the plan of God. He wrote that Jesus was the "lamb without blemish or spot" (1 Pet. 1:19) who was "foreknown before the foundation of the world but was made manifest in the last times for the sake of you" (1 Pet. 1:20). God planned redemption before creation. And at the ordained time, the chosen rescuer came. Jesus laid down his life as the sacrificial Lamb of God.

Conclusion

Speaking hundreds of years before Jesus died on the cross, Isaiah said, "Yet it was the will of the LORD to crush him" (Isa. 53:10). Did the divine plan remove the culpability of the wicked men who wanted to put Jesus to death? No, for Peter told his Jerusalem audience that they crucified and killed Jesus (Acts 2:23). And later, during a prayer, the disciples said that "truly in this city there were gathered together against your holy servant Jesus, whom you anointed, both Herod and Pontius Pilate, along with the Gentiles and the peoples of Israel, to do whatever your hand and your plan had predestined to take place" (Acts 4:27–28). Yet the greatest truth about the cross was its divine ordination. The disciples certainly viewed the cross differently after Jesus's resurrection, yet beyond their perspectives stood the eternal divine plan. And this plan centered on Christ Jesus, whose crucifixion and resurrection were for the praise of God's grace and glory.

2

OUR HELPLESS ESTATE

For the good news about Jesus to shine with all its brilliance, there is bad news we must hear first. Fair warning: the bad news levels us so low that we can't lift ourselves from the helpless state of sin. But if we don't believe the bad news about ourselves, why is the gospel worth proclaiming or believing?

Wanting to Be Like God

Things are not the way they should be. In Genesis 1, God made the world where he would unfold his Christ-centered plan. In Genesis 2, God made Adam and Eve to dwell in fellowship with him. In the beginning, there was no sin or shame. But in Genesis 3, Adam and Eve rebelled against God, and "the fall" occurred. The descent was devastating.

Here's what happened. In God's abundant goodness and wisdom, he provided for his image-bearers and gave them every tree in the Garden of Eden for food (Gen. 2:16), all the trees except one—the tree of the knowledge of good and evil (Gen. 2:9). God commanded that they must not eat from that tree, and his command came with a warning that "in the day that you eat of it you shall surely die" (Gen. 2:17).

Never to waste an opportunity, Satan approached Eve with an appealing deception. He initiated dialogue about the trees of the garden. Eve told the serpent about God's prohibition and warning (Gen. 3:3), but the serpent insisted, "You will not surely die. For God knows that when you eat of it your eyes will be opened, and you will be like God, knowing good and evil"

(Gen. 3:4–5). *God is misleading you. He doesn't want you to have his knowledge. He's holding out on you. Don't you want to be like God?*

As Michael Horton explains, "Satan's first strategy was to persuade Eve that God was stingy and narrow-minded....The assumption is that God is just keeping us down, holding us back from realizing our inner potential and divinity."[1] Satan's strategy succeeded, and Eve disobeyed God and ate fruit from the tree. She gave some to Adam, and he ate it, too (Gen 3:6). We should stop for a dramatic pause. God had given the couple everything that was good. He gave them dominion over his creation and commanded them to multiply (Gen. 1:26–28). But here in the Garden of Eden, the enemy successfully tempted Adam and Eve to go against their Creator.

In wanting to be like God, Adam and Eve fell short of everything God created them to be. This was the first occasion of humans putting self in the place of God, choosing human wisdom over God's and ignoring God's good command for a more appealing alternative. This alternative changed everything. What should God have done in response to their disobedience?

A Blind Eye on a Holy God?

Growing up in church, I remember hearing the story of the garden rebellion and wondering, *Why couldn't God just let them off the hook and pretend it never happened?* Perhaps you've wondered something similar. It seems like God could have avoided the whole mess if he'd just swept their disobedience under the rug and kept them in the Garden of Eden.

But a holy God can't turn a blind eye. God couldn't ignore such transgression and still remain worthy of worship. You can't separate the worthiness of God from the splendor and glory of his righteousness. God is right in himself, and he always does what is right. To never compromise his righteousness and justice, God never acts in ways that are contrary to the greatest display of his glory and name. God would be devaluing his glory and name if he didn't act righteously with Adam and Eve.

---

1. Michael Horton, *The Gospel-Driven Life: Being Good News People in a Bad News World* (Grand Rapids, MI: Baker Books, 2009), 112.

Since Adam and Eve asserted themselves as moral authorities in the universe and wanted the wisdom of God apart from obedience to God, the perfect righteousness of God demanded that he keep his word of warning to them. He had promised that the lawbreaker would surely die. So did God promise something and not follow through? His trustworthiness is on the line.

God pronounced judgment, and you should expect a holy and righteous God to do nothing less. If a human judge let a guilty murderer go free without any repercussion, people would be outraged, and the media would expose the judge's profane character. People would demand that the judge surrender his or her seat. They would claim that the judge tarnished the meaning of justice, and the judge's unrighteous act would stain his or her name. How much more, then, must God deal justly for the sake of his name in the universe. He doesn't play fast and loose with his commands. God warned that there would be judgment if anyone ate the fruit of that tree, so judgment there must be. God will not compromise his righteousness for people.

First, God judged the serpent, Satan (Rev. 12:9), who tempted Eve. In God's judgment was the promise of a future descendant from Eve who would crush the head of the serpent (Gen. 3:15). Second, God judged Eve (Gen. 3:16). Third, God judged Adam (Gen. 3:17–19). After God pronounced these judgments, something else happened. "The LORD God made for Adam and for his wife garments of skins and clothed them" (Gen. 3:21). God judged Adam and Eve and then covered their shame with garments that he himself provided. The provision of these garments of skin implied the death of an animal. Pictured in Genesis 3:21 is the holy God covering the shame of sinners with sacrifice.

To display his uncompromising righteousness, God must judge sin, not turn a blind eye. And for there to be any hope for transgressors, God must provide a covering (an *atonement*) for sin. In the early chapters of the Bible, we are glimpsing the themes of judgment and grace. These twin themes are like rivers intertwining throughout the Bible, meeting climactically at the cross of Jesus.

The Groaning Universe

Sin has broken us, and broken people live in a broken world that needs redemption. Paul depicted creation as anticipating liberation.

> *For the creation waits with eager longing for the revealing of the sons of God. For the creation was subjected to futility, not willingly, but because of him who subjected it, in hope that the creation itself will be set free from its bondage to corruption and obtain the freedom of the glory of the children of God.*

—Rom. 8:19–21

The one who subjected creation is God, and the purpose of its subjection is its ultimate liberation from bondage. We live between the tragedy of Genesis 3 and the transformation of Revelation 21 and 22. Christians should reflect on how the horrors of sin have affected everything around us. The world is full of frustration and toil. Plants wither, animals die, and thorns grow along the cursed ground (Gen. 3:17–18). Disasters such as earthquakes, floods, and hurricanes occur throughout the world. If creation groans through these travails and tragedies, how much greater must be the heinousness of our sins to God. The broken world testifies to our depravity and disobedience. The judgments God administered have fractured all creation.

But remember, the subjection of creation was for the sake of redemption. Creation groans, and those groans will be heard. Creation is groaning like someone in the pains of childbirth (Rom. 8:22). Like childbirth, the pains and groans of this world will give way to a wonderful reality when God completes his work of redemption. God will make his blessings flow, as far as the curse is found. The groans of creation are not in vain. The day of cosmic redemption is sure.

A God of Holy Wrath

Maybe you agree that sin is awful, but do you wonder if the divine judgment in Genesis 3 was an outrageous overreaction? Due to our sinfulness, we cannot fully comprehend our sinfulness. Add to that this truth: we don't understand the holiness of God. If we understood the holiness of God and how outrageous and terrible sin is, we would see that God is justifiably angry with sinful people. God has never overreacted to anything.

While for most people holiness means moral perfection, calling God holy means more than saying he lacks any moral flaw. The idea behind holiness is to be *set apart*. God is set apart from his creation in the sense that he is different, or wholly other, than what he has made. But he's not set apart on a level playing field. He is set apart and *above* what he has made. God is transcendent. R. C. Sproul said, "When the Bible calls God holy, it means primarily that God is transcendentally separate."[2] Pay close attention to God's words in Isaiah 40:25: "To whom then will you compare me, that I should be like him?" The answer is *no one*. If we were to search all creation, we would find no one equal to the Holy One. God's separateness puts his character in another category. As Sproul put it, "The word *holy* calls attention to all that God is. It reminds us that His love is holy love, His justice is holy justice, His mercy is holy mercy."[3]

Thinking about God's holiness prepares us to think about his wrath. As a holy and just God, he would not simply let wickedness go without a response. God's wrath is his *righteous anger provoked by sin*. According to D. A. Carson, "In itself, wrath, unlike love, is *not* one of the intrinsic perfections of God. Rather, it is a function of God's holiness against sin. Where there is no sin, there is no wrath."[4] The idea of God's anger being *righteous* is important, because the anger we manifest is rarely a righteous kind. When Paul commands believers, "In your anger do not sin" (Eph. 4:26 NIV), his command shows that being angry is not necessarily equivalent to sinning. One can be righteously angry.

According to Psalm 2, God is righteously angry when worldly powers oppose him (Ps. 2:2). He "will terrify them in his fury" (Ps. 2:5). The

---

2. R. C. Sproul, *The Holiness of God*, 2nd Ed. (Wheaton, IL: Tyndale House, 1998), 38.
3. Ibid., 40.
4. D. A. Carson, *The Difficult Doctrine of the Love of God* (Wheaton, IL: Crossway Books, 2000), 67.

psalmist warns readers, "Kiss the Son, lest he be angry, and you perish in the way, for his wrath is quickly kindled" (Ps. 2:12). Paul tells his readers that "the wrath of God is revealed from heaven against all ungodliness and unrighteousness of men, who by their unrighteousness suppress the truth" (Rom. 1:18). God is even now, in a true sense, pouring out his wrath. The Bible also promises a future day of God's wrath that will surpass any preceding judgment (2 Thess. 1:7–10).

Rather than offering worldwide worship to God's holy name, people have provoked the wrath of God by their disobedience and idolatry. Yes, God is compassionate and gracious, slow to anger and abounding in love (Exod. 34:6). But his anger does rise, and he will not leave the guilty unpunished (Exod. 34:7). God's anger is pure, uncompromised, and righteous. His wrath is holy, terrible, and just. God is not angry at sin because he's unholy. God is angry at sin because he *is* holy. As a righteous God, he should be angry at sin. As a holy God worthy of worldwide worship and adoration from the nations, he should uphold the value of his name and the weight of his glory by meting out judgment against the unrighteous.

While sinners now disdainfully spurn God's name and live as if he does not matter, such mockery will not be the final word. God will have the last word, a word of justice appointed for the day of God's wrath (Rom. 2:5). On that day when the dust settles, the wicked will not stand.

Righteous and Loving

God's judgment does not contradict the truth that God is love. Does divine judgment seem unloving to you? If we define love—or anything about God—solely from our perspective, the result will be a deity of our own design. If we don't think certain actions are appropriate for God, we will disregard them. If biblical truths make us uncomfortable, we will reword them or reject them. Carson observes, "The love of God in our culture has been purged of anything the culture finds uncomfortable. The love of God has been sanitized, democratized, and above all sentimentalized."[5]

---

5. Ibid., 11.

Submission to God's Word means to humbly receive—from the top down—the revelation from God about who he is. Knowing God does not begin with our instincts or preferences or preconceived notions. Knowing God means believing what he has said about himself in the scriptures. And in the scriptures, God never pits his righteousness against his love. God is love (1 John 4:16), and God is righteous (Ps. 11:7). We must affirm and believe all that God reveals about himself to rightly understand him. Love and righteousness are not parts of who God is. His attributes cannot be separated into isolated categories. Paul Wells writes, "God's love is not God's love unless it is eternal, true, righteous, and all the other aspects of his nature that characterize him as God."[6] There is no tension within God, no warring attributes.

The final judgment of sinners, therefore, is not unloving. Despite the common objection, a loving God will send people to hell. God himself defines what it means for him to act in loving ways. We must guard against projecting our notions about love onto God's holy character. Herein is God's love, "that while we were still sinners, Christ died for us" (Rom. 5:8). The cross is the grand demonstration of divine love, where the Son of God died for the enemies of God.

Two Heads

Apart from Christ, we are rebels who love the darkness. We have all offended God's holiness and provoked his righteousness. We are born into this world depraved and sinful, not neutral or innocent. Our natural bent is not *toward* God but *away* from him. Instead of worshiping God as he deserves, we worship what he has made. His blessings and common graces become our idols. We elevate good things to the place where only God is worthy, simultaneously corrupting those good things and dishonoring God.

Our inward spiritual condition is connected to the representative of humanity, our head named Adam. The first man's disobedience affected

---

6. Paul Wells, *Cross Words: The Biblical Doctrine of the Atonement* (Scotland: Christian Focus Publications, 2006), 55.

more than just him because he was the representative of the human race. When Adam acted, he acted for all of us. Sin entered the world through one man (Rom. 5:12). The result of Adam's trespass was condemnation for all people (Rom. 5:18). Through his disobedience, "the many were made sinners" (Rom. 5:19).

As head and representative of humanity, Adam bore a special responsibility. Though God warned Adam that eating from the tree of the knowledge of good and evil would bring death (Gen. 2:17), Adam took the fruit that Eve gave him and ate it (Gen. 3:6). When both Adam and Eve disobeyed, God first spoke to Adam: "Where are you?" (Gen. 3:9). God asked this question not for himself but for Adam, to draw the guilty one into the open. When God was outlining the judgment for Adam, he prefaced it by saying, "Because you have listened to the voice of your wife and have eaten of the tree of which I commanded you, 'You shall not eat of it,' cursed is the ground because of you; in pain you shall eat of it all the days of your life" (Gen. 3:17). Adam should have led in the way of righteousness, but instead he followed in the path of disobedience. Rather than acting as the righteous representative of humanity, he disobeyed his Creator's command.

However, since Jesus was the slain Lamb in the Father's pre-creation plan, the story of redemption had already incorporated the fall of humanity. Adam was a pattern of the one to come (Rom. 5:14). Adam was a pattern or type of Christ in this way: they were both representative heads, Adam being the head of old creation and Christ being the head of new creation. Whereas sin flowed to "many" through Adam, God's grace flowed through the "one man Jesus Christ" (Rom. 5:15). Adam's disobedience in the Garden of Eden brought condemnation, but Jesus's obedience on the cross brought justification (Rom. 5:16, 18–19). Death reigned through Adam, but everlasting life reigns through Jesus (Rom. 5:17). Adam and Christ are both representative heads, but their different acts brought about very different effects.

Dead in Adam

As people descending from the line of Adam, we are *in Adam*. And Paul said "in Adam all die" (1 Cor. 15:22). Being in Adam means that our spiritual status derives from the Genesis 3 events. We not only sin, but we are "made sinners" (Rom. 5:19). Our orientation and inclinations are bound up with our earthly father. Paul told the Ephesians that before salvation, "you were dead in the trespasses and sins" (Eph. 2:1), which is a further description of what it means to be in Adam. To be in Adam is to be spiritually dead.

The fall of humanity affected people at the deepest level—their minds. Paul says that unbelievers were "carrying out the desires of the body and the mind" (Eph. 2:3). With our minds we think about and desire what dishonors God. Our hearts are deceptive, ill beyond cure (Jer. 17:9). Cultural phrases like "follow your heart" are terrible news when we realize, as Michael Horton points out, that "our hearts are in love with that which will ultimately destroy us."[7] A depraved mind is part of God's righteous judgment (Rom. 1:28).

We sin because we are sinners. Jesus identifies the heart of the problem: the *heart*. He said that "what comes out of the mouth proceeds from the heart, and this defiles a person. For out of the heart come evil thoughts, murder, adultery, sexual immorality, theft, false witness, slander" (Matt. 15:18–19). When scripture talks about the corruption of the mind and the wickedness of the heart, essentially the same human faculty is in view—the faculty of our will, desires, and inclinations.

Our sinful nature desires what is contrary to the Spirit (Gal. 5:17–21). As humans with a sinful nature, our desires are not easily suppressed. Yet sinners do not live out as much sin as they could. People may restrain themselves from certain transgressions because of social and legal pressures. Apart from the work of Christ in our hearts, we are totally depraved, but that doesn't mean we are as bad as we could be. Being depraved means that sin has dominion over all the faculties of the unbeliever. Sin is a reigning power

---

7. Horton, *The Gospel-Driven Life*, 75.

in the body of the unbeliever (Rom. 6:12), as well as a cruel master that deceives and destroys (Rom. 6:14, 16, 21).

The Bible also describes our spiritual deadness in terms of light and darkness. Jesus said, "The light has come into the world, and people loved the darkness rather than the light because their works were evil. For everyone who does wicked things hates the light and does not come to the light, lest his works should be exposed" (John 3:19–20). If we are dead in Adam, we will love the darkness instead of the light. Unaided by the Holy Spirit, unbelievers don't long for the light; they cherish the darkness because it covers their wicked deeds. Unbelievers don't yearn for righteousness; they pursue iniquity. Unbelievers don't want to please God; they want to please themselves.

Though dead in Adam, people still love, long for, and worship things— but the objects of all our affections are our wicked deeds, not God. Sinners have replaced God with what is not God. They have "exchanged the glory of the immortal God" for other things (Rom. 1:23). In place of the truth, they have embraced falsehood (Rom. 1:25). This is man-centeredness and idolatry. The state of sinful people is futile thinking and foolish hearts (Rom. 1:21). This descent into depravity was—and is—horrific.

So, if sinful people don't worship God, glorify God, esteem God, or obey God, what does that mean? Paul gives the verdict: everyone is "under sin" (Rom. 3:9). Being in Adam and being under sin are two ways of describing our helpless estate. Being under sin means that there is no one righteous and no one who seeks God (Rom. 3:10–11). What about other religions? Doesn't the prevalence of spirituality show that people are seeking God? Other religions are not evidence of people seeking God; they're evidence of people fleeing from God. Remember, Paul said that sinners have exchanged God's truth for a lie (Rom. 1:25). Unbelievers aren't pursuing truth; they're living in deception. Idolaters aren't secretly worshiping God when they bow down to a lifeless idol; they're sinning against their Creator who is worthy of their praise.

Lacking knowledge of the true and living God, unbelievers are blind to the gospel of Christ. "In their case the god of this world has blinded the minds of the unbelievers, to keep them from seeing the light of the gospel of the glory of Christ, who is the image of God" (2 Cor. 4:4). Normally, you would speak about blind eyes—but blind *minds*? According to Paul, understanding something is seeing with our minds. And if we don't understand the glorious gospel of Jesus Christ, then our minds are blind.

The news about our condition is deeply disturbing. Unbelievers cannot see the light of the gospel—their only hope—and they naturally reject the light because they love the darkness in which they dwell. In other words, unbelievers can't see the gospel, and they don't want to see the gospel. Sin affects both ability and desire. To underscore this point, the narrator of John's Gospel explains why many Jews rejected Jesus, even though he had done miraculous signs in their presence. The Jews would not believe in him (John 12:37), and they could not believe in him (John 12:39). It's both: they *won't*, and they *can't*.

Incapable and Accountable

If sinners can't and won't embrace the light of the gospel on their own, why are sinners still accountable to God? Why is God still angry with sinners if they are in such a helpless spiritual state? The presupposition in the questions is that if sinners are no longer *able* to do something (in this case, embrace the gospel on their own), they are no longer *obligated* to do it.

Let's first establish that God does hold sinners accountable. "Now we know that whatever the law says it speaks to those who are under the law, so that every mouth may be stopped, and the whole world may be held accountable to God" (Rom. 3:19). God doesn't hold only Jews or only Gentiles accountable; the whole world must answer to him. No one can boast in their righteousness before a holy God.

But showing that sinners are accountable to God doesn't make the problem go away—arguably, it makes the problem worse. Jesus said, "No one can come to me unless the Father who sent me draws him" (John 6:44), and "no one can come to me unless it is granted him by the Father" (John 6:65). In John 6, coming to Jesus means believing in him (John 6:35). According to Jesus, sinners are unable to believe in him on their own. Yet the inability of the sinner doesn't remove the command or obligation to believe in Jesus. In fact, Jesus never says that no one can come to him and that he's going to stop telling people to come to him. He never says that because of the fall of humanity, sinners are unable to obey God's will on their own, so he's changing the rules. God cannot change the rules because the obligation of sinners has nothing to do with any criteria outside God that he could change. There is no standard outside God—he *is* the standard. God is worthy of worship, whether or not sinners are able to worship him. God is worthy of trust, whether or not sinners are able to trust him. God is worthy of obedience, whether or not sinners are able to obey him. *God is worthy*, and that is the point.

The sinner's problem is with God himself, not with any rules he has set up external to himself. We have become unable, but God has not become unworthy. The issue of whether sinners are accountable to a holy God can be settled not by implying human ability but by affirming the supreme worth of God. When we see that God is worthy of worship and obedience from all humanity, the obligation to worship him is no longer dependent on what sinners are able to do after Genesis 3. Because God doesn't change, the duty to worship and obey him doesn't change either.

We are wrong if we assume that God would never command us to do something we are unable to do. In fact, throughout the redemptive storyline in the Old Testament, a major theme is Israel's inability to keep the law God gave them to obey. God never rescinded his law, even though Israel failed to keep it. In a scene of irony, God gave Moses his law on Mount Sinai while the Israelites were worshiping a golden calf at the bottom of the mountain (Exod. 32:1–6). The first commandment said, "You shall have no other gods before me" (Exod. 20:3), yet the Israelites worshiped a golden calf instead of the true and living God. They couldn't keep the very first commandment.

Paul confirms the sinner's inability to obey God's law: "For the mind that is set on the flesh is hostile to God, for it does not submit to God's law; indeed, it cannot" (Rom. 8:7). The sinner *doesn't* and *cannot* submit to

God's law. The sinner doesn't desire to obey God and lacks the ability to obey him. It's not unwillingness or inability—it's *both*.

We are accountable to God because he is God, and he does not change. He is worthy of worldwide adoration, worship, and obedience. The epic tragedy is the failure and inability of sinful people to fulfill such God-honoring and soul-satisfying duties. But God will not devalue the worth of his glory because of human inability. He will not lower his expectations, he will not change the rules, and he will not give sinners a passing grade for doing their spiritual best.

Maybe the truth about our spiritual incapability and accountability makes you think of someone with an unkind and unreasonable expectation. Would you demand an embrace from an armless person? Would you expect a blind person to drive a car well? The problem with those illustrations, though, is that they are physical illustrations addressing a spiritual truth, and sometimes physical analogies are inadequate. Our obligation and inability to honor God as he deserves is not a matter of physical handicap. There's no moral obligation to give hugs or drive cars. Given the history of Israel in the Old Testament, would we really want to say that God only gives commands according to our abilities? Did God send Jesus to the cross simply because sinners were unwilling to obey his law? Or did Jesus die because sinners were unable to fulfill God's requirements—requirements he was nevertheless right to have?

The law reveals our sin and our inability to keep God's commands. Paul wrote, "For by works of the law no human being will be justified in his sight, since through the law comes knowledge of sin" (Rom. 3:20). The law exacerbates the sin problem; it doesn't curb it. "Now the law came in to increase the trespass, but where sin increased, grace abounded all the more" (Rom. 5:20). We are morally obligated yet morally unable to obey our righteous and holy God.

Conclusion

The good news of the gospel will only be received as good once we believe the bad news about our sinful condition before a holy God. We come into this world dead in Adam. We must reckon with the righteousness of God and with our sin-loving selves that are bent toward rebellion and unbelief. We love the darkness because we are unwilling and unable to love the light. With blind minds and darkened hearts, we deserve the condemnation of God and have no strength or amount of works to earn a right standing with God. Yet as the hymn writer wrote, "Christ hath regarded my helpless estate, and hath shed His own blood for my soul."[8]

---

8. Horatio Spafford, "It Is Well with My Soul," in "The American Colony in Jerusalem: A Family Tragedy," *Library of Congress*, https://www.loc.gov/exhibits/americancolony/amcolony -family.html.

3

GOD THE JUST AND JUSTIFIER

Given the terrible problem of our sin and given the unwavering righteousness of the living God, let us wonder how it is that sinners could ever be forgiven. For God to pardon his enemies and reconcile them into fellowship and eternal peace, surely we have arrived at an intractable problem. How can mercy ever be right for God to give? On what basis are the unrighteous declared righteous? The cross of Jesus Christ is the solution to the problem and is the basis of our pardon. God's wrath and mercy meet at the cross.

The Problem of Forgiveness

Our greatest need is to be right with God because sin has alienated us from spiritual fellowship and union with him. Dead in Adam, we deserve holy wrath. God is worthy of worship, which we have given to lesser things. Forgiving sinners is a problem because God is *righteous*. He can't just say, "You're forgiven," and move on. The book of Proverbs tells us, "He who justifies the wicked and he who condemns the righteous are both alike an abomination to the LORD" (Prov. 17:15).

When the Bible names something an abomination, pause and take notice. It is abominable to justify the wicked. When the guilty go free, God detests it. Innocent people do not deserve a guilty verdict; the guilty should pay for the wicked deeds they commit. Do you see how Proverbs 17:15 sets up our dilemma regarding the gospel? The Christian announcement is that God justifies *the ungodly*.

25

We are guilty of breaking God's law, pursuing idols, esteeming ourselves instead of glorifying God, and bucking divine authority in exchange for human independence. We have committed cosmic treason. We are guilty as charged. If a judge simply releases a guilty criminal back onto the streets unpunished, people cry out for real justice and impugn the character of that judge. Yet people may simply assume that God should be forgiving, and they see no problem with a righteous and holy God pardoning wicked rebels. It's like we expect divine forgiveness.

Have you considered the problem of God actually forgiving sinners? If honorable, earthly judges don't release criminals without a basis of innocence, how can God ever pardon the ungodly? God even describes himself as one "who will by no means clear the guilty" (Exod. 34:7). If he acquits the ungodly without a legitimate basis, then he is no better than an earthly judge who receives bribes, plays favorites, or simply doesn't care about justice. Such a God would not be worthy of worship, for he would be unrighteous, unholy.

Surprised at the Wrong Thing

According to Romans 4:5, God is the one "who justifies the ungodly." God does the very thing Proverbs 17:15 assures us that he detests. How can this be?

Maybe after further investigation into the matter, God discovers that some sinners are not guilty, and so he acquits them. You've probably read stories about inmates going free after DNA tests vindicated their innocence. But that scenario doesn't parallel our spiritual condition. God is holy, and there is no one righteous, not one (Rom. 3:11–12).

Perhaps God justifies the wicked by changing his requirements, like a teacher who wants to pass a near-failing student. The teacher makes the final exam easier so the student passes. So does God take his law less seriously so sinners can be justified? Surely not! This would introduce a host of other theological problems, such as God devaluing his name and compromising his righteousness. The standards don't change because God *is* the standard. God cannot modify his worth to admit the guilty into his presence. So much for lowering the bar of divine righteousness.

Yet God must have a basis for this outrageous act of justifying the ungodly. The gospel announces that the basis of God's justification of sinners is the work of Jesus Christ on the cross (Gal. 2:16). God has made a way through Jesus by which his justice is satisfied and sinners are forgiven. This news is what makes grace amazing. It makes mercy precious. It makes heaven hopeful.

Christians need a thorough review of the basis for justification so they might praise God for his kindness and grace. Paul says that "God, being rich in mercy, because of the great love with which he loved us, even when we were dead in our trespasses, made us alive together with Christ—by grace you have been saved" (Eph. 2:4–5).

Some people aren't surprised at God's kindness. They sort of expect it, even if they don't admit it out loud. God's *judgment* surprises them, though. They may even scowl at the thought of divine wrath and wonder why God is so worked up. They may dismiss God's wrath as that old hell-fire-and-brimstone idea that many people don't really believe anymore. In their minds, the love of God cancels out the wrath of God. These people expect heaven, and they despise the idea of hell.

The tragedy is that we are surprised at the wrong thing. In view of God's holiness and righteousness, and because each of us has committed cosmic treason in our rebellion against our Creator, we should expect judgment. Greg Gilbert is right: "We Christians have done a bang-up job convincing the world that God loves them. But if we're going to understand just how glorious and life-giving the gospel of Jesus Christ is, we have to understand that this loving and compassionate God is also holy and righteous, and that he is determined never to overlook, ignore, or tolerate sin."[1] Rather than being surprised at the thought of sinners going to hell, we should be astounded that anyone goes to heaven.

---

1. Greg Gilbert, *What Is the Gospel?* (Wheaton, IL: Crossway, 2010), 45.

Generations of Bloody Sacrifices

Do you know how the cross accomplished redemption for sinners? Have you ever wondered why Jesus had to die instead of God simply announcing from heaven, "Believe in my Son, and you'll be saved from the penalty of your sins"? The New Testament reveals the meaning and message of the cross. The gospel is a cross-centered message. We will not understand the gospel if the purpose of the cross remains unclear. We have to talk about Jesus sacrificing himself in our place.

The cross didn't introduce the notion of sacrifice. God covered the shame of Adam and Eve with the skin of a sacrificed animal (Gen. 3:21). And as the Israelites prepared to leave Egypt, the event of Passover occurred when God didn't judge those who covered the sides and tops of their door-frames with the blood of a slaughtered lamb (Exod. 12:5–13). The Lord said, "The blood shall be a sign for you, on the houses where you are. And when I see the blood, I will pass over you, and no plague will befall you to destroy you, when I strike the land of Egypt" (Exod. 12:13). In Leviticus 16, the Lord gave instructions to Moses about the Day of Atonement. "For on this day shall atonement be made for you to cleanse you. You shall be clean before the LORD from all your sins" (Lev. 16:30). Reflecting on these Old Testament concepts, the author of Hebrews wrote that "without the shedding of blood there is no forgiveness of sins" (Heb. 9:22).

Israel's tabernacle and temple were bloody places. The Lord beheld countless sacrifices as the generations passed. What did all this death signify? These bloody rituals pointed to the heinous nature of sin and reminded the people of its punishment. In Genesis 2:17, God warned Adam that if he ate from the tree of the knowledge of good and evil, he would surely die. Death was punishment. And following the fall of humanity, death was the pattern.

Sacrifices didn't point only to physical death as a punishment for sin. They signified the *spiritual* aspect of God's judgment. Paul explained that "the wages of sin is death, but the free gift of God is eternal life in Christ Jesus our Lord" (Rom. 6:23). Paul contrasted spiritual death with spiritual life. Spiritual death is the wage earned by the sinner. But when God grants spiritual life, it's not because the sinner has earned it. Sinners find in Christ what they could never earn.

A problem with the Old Testament sacrificial system was the unending need for sacrifice. It seemed that if things remained as they did, followers of God would be forever offering sacrifices for their sins. Continual offerings were necessary because no sacrifice was perfect or completely effective.

Coming to an End

God instituted the Old Testament sacrificial system to provide temporary covering of sin until his unfolding redemptive plan climaxed with the death of Jesus. To bring an end to an imperfect system of insufficient sacrifices, there needed to be a perfect sacrifice. It was always God's intention to send Jesus, for Jesus was the slain Lamb before all creation, marked with the mission of dying on the cross.

If no one could ever provide a perfect and sufficient sacrifice for sins, then someone other than a sinner would have to offer a satisfactory sacrifice. And since the Old Testament sacrifices for sins required the death of animals, the final sacrifice offered for sins would require nothing less than death. C. S. Lewis argued it this way: "But supposing God became a man—suppose our human nature which can suffer and die was amalgamated with God's nature in one person—then that person could help us. He could surrender His will, and suffer and die, because He was man; and He could do it perfectly because He was God."[2]

God sent Jesus so "he might taste death for everyone" (Heb. 2:9). Since people are flesh and blood, Jesus himself "likewise partook of the same things, that through death he might destroy the one who has the power of death, that is, the devil" (Heb. 2:14). By taking on flesh, the Son of God was able to become a merciful and faithful high priest for sinners (Heb. 2:17). The Old Testament high priest made atonement for the sins of Israel on a special day each year—aptly named the Day of Atonement. Year after year, and high priest after high priest, God covered the sins of the people

---

2. C. S. Lewis, *Mere Christianity* (New York: Touchstone, 1952), 60–61.

throughout the generations. But no perfect sacrifice appeared until Jesus. Death prevented the Old Testament priests from continuing in office, but the resurrection of Jesus established his permanent priesthood (Heb. 7:23–27).

Jesus "appeared once for all at the end of the ages to put away sin by the sacrifice of himself" (Heb. 9:26). Temporary atonement gave way to a permanent, fully accomplished work. The high priest performed his rituals in Leviticus 16 once a year, but Jesus accomplished atonement once for all. While hanging on the cross, Jesus said, "It is finished," right before he died (John 19:30). Confirming what Jesus had accomplished, the curtain of the temple tore from top to bottom (Mark 15:38), the curtain that separated the presence of God from the people of God. The temple was finished. The sacrifices were over. Jesus was the new temple and the final sacrifice.

Atonement through Substitution

In the Old Testament, the sacrificed animals were substitutes. On the Day of Atonement, God told Moses that "Aaron shall lay both his hands on the head of the live goat, and confess over it all the iniquities of the people of Israel, and all their transgressions, all their sins" (Lev. 16:21). As a substitute for the Israelites, the goat bore their sins and fled to the desert, symbolically carrying away the sins of the people (Lev. 16:22).

The notion of substitution is integral to the New Testament's teaching about Jesus's death. "When we give attention and authority to all parts of the New Testament canon, substitution becomes the center and focus of the Bible's witness to the meaning of Christ's death, and the measure of God's redeeming love."[3] Jesus did not die for his own sins. The Son of God was not a sinner. Rather, God "made him to be sin who knew no sin, so that in him we might become the righteousness of God" (2 Cor. 5:21). Since the Son of God had no sin of his own, he could perfectly bear ours.

Paul considered the teaching of Christ's substitutionary death as a matter of first importance for the early Christians: "For I delivered to you as of first

---

3. J. I. Packer, and Mark Dever, *In My Place Condemned He Stood: Celebrating the Glory of the Atonement* (Wheaton, IL: Crossway Books, 2007), 109–110.

importance what I also received: that Christ died for our sins in accordance with the Scriptures" (1 Cor. 15:3). Notice that the scriptures foretold not only his death but also its substitutionary nature. Perhaps Paul was thinking of phrases from Isaiah 53: "Surely he has borne our griefs and carried our sorrows; yet we esteemed him stricken, smitten by God, and afflicted. But he was pierced for our transgressions; he was crushed for our iniquities; upon him was the chastisement that brought us peace, and with his wounds we are healed" (Isa. 53:4–5). Jesus died bearing the sin of sinners.

Sinners dead in transgression have no ability to save themselves. We were powerless enemies of God (Rom. 5:6, 10). The substitutionary death of Jesus for enemies of God is a graphic illustration of God's love: "God shows his love for us in that while we were still sinners, Christ died for us" (Rom. 5:8). In Peter's words, Jesus's death for sinners was "the righteous" dying "for the unrighteous" (1 Pet. 3:18). He laid down his life when we were helpless, not when we had gone most of the way back to God in our own strength.

When the biblical authors talk about Jesus dying as a substitute for sinners, they teach that Jesus bore the penalty for our sin—divine judgment. This is known as the *penal-substitutionary* understanding of the cross. The penalty-bearing reality of Jesus's death is essential to understand the saving function of Jesus's death. Understanding that Christ bore the wrath of God is the core teaching of the cross event and the gospel. If we marginalize or ignore the penal-substitutionary nature of Jesus's death, we gut the gospel of its good news for sinners.

We need to know what happened on the cross, the redemptive work that results in a verdict of justification for every sinner who believes in Jesus. We must talk again about God's judgment because, as Michael Horton puts it, "at the heart of Christ's work on the cross is his propitiation of God's wrath."[4] If we don't first understand God's righteous wrath upon our sin, we will not think much of the good news of Christ dying as our wrath-satisfying substitute.

---

4. Horton, *The Gospel-Driven Life*, 51.

God is not an uninterested third party regarding the subject of human sin. The judge of the universe is the one against whom we have committed cosmic treason and idolatry. And the King of the universe doesn't shrug off such rebellion. Cosmic treason incurs divine judgment, and such a penalty is the obstacle to divine forgiveness, which is why a penal-substitutionary understanding of the cross is so important. "Penal substitution, as an idea, presupposes a penalty...due to us from God the Judge for wrong done and failure to meet his claims."[5] The penal-substitutionary death of Jesus makes reconciliation with God possible. Paul's message was that in Christ "God was reconciling the world to himself, not counting their trespasses against them" (2 Cor. 5:19).

Forgiving sinners is how God reconciles them to himself. If there is no way for the world's righteous judge to forgive sinners, they will remain unreconciled and under wrath, for sinners are by nature objects of wrath (Eph. 2:3). Those who don't believe in Jesus are condemned already (John 3:18, 36). How can a righteous God simply stop counting sins against wrath-deserving sinners? God counted the sins of the world against Christ so that anyone who trusts in Christ for salvation can receive forgiveness.

The Most Important Paragraph in the Bible

Martin Luther once described Romans 3:21–26 as the most important part of the Bible. At the beginning of this passage, Paul announced the good news that the world was waiting for: "But now the righteousness of God has been manifested apart from the law, although the Law and the Prophets bear witness to it" (Rom. 3:21). The word *righteousness* here refers to the saving act of God that justifies sinners. God has a way of declaring sinners *not guilty*. This verdict of justification occurs "apart from the law" because no one can perfectly obey God's law. The law only exacerbates our sin (Rom. 5:20). Our only hope for justification is a legal declaration made apart from the law.

Paul wrote that justification comes "through faith in Jesus Christ for all who believe" (Rom. 3:22). God isn't biased toward any ethnicities or other external criteria when it comes to his verdict of justification, "for all have

---

5. Packer and Dever, *In My Place Condemned He Stood*, 82.

sinned and fall short of the glory of God" (Rom. 3:23). Since all have sinned and deserve God's judgment, all are equally unworthy of forgiveness.

Paul gives the basis for God's justification of sinners: they are "justified by his grace as a gift, through the redemption that is in Christ Jesus" (Rom. 3:24). This is a loaded verse. God justifies by grace. It is God's grace, not the sinner's merits, that leads to justification. God's verdict of *no condemnation* comes to sinners on the basis of Christ's redemptive work.

Romans 3:25–26 is the climax of this important paragraph. God put forward his Son "as a propitiation by his blood, to be received by faith" (Rom. 3:25). To propitiate someone means to turn aside their wrath. Jesus was the propitiation for sinners under God's wrath. Jesus has turned aside divine wrath for all who believe in him, satisfying the justice of God on the cross. Through faith in Christ, God justifies the sinner and reckons the sacrifice of Jesus as a sufficient propitiation for holy wrath.

It is worth quoting J. I. Packer at length here:

> Has the word *propitiation* any place in your Christianity? In the faith of the New Testament it is central. The love of God, the taking of human form by the Son, the meaning of the cross, Christ's heavenly intercession, the way of salvation—all are to be explained in terms of it…and any explanation from which the thought of propitiation is missing will be incomplete, and indeed actually misleading, by New Testament standards.[6]

Paul expands on why God poured out wrath on his Son: "to show God's righteousness, because in his divine forbearance he had passed over former sins" (Rom. 3:25). In view of all the unpunished wickedness in the world, God appeared to be unjust. He had not punished sin as it fully deserved, and his judgment was not yet as comprehensive as the wickedness itself. God had left himself open to charges of unrighteousness and injustice. And many people throughout the ages have pointed to the evil in the world and concluded that no holy and good God could possibly exist.

---

6. J. I. Packer, *Knowing God* (Downers Grove, IL: InterVarsity Press, 1973), 181.

The problem of evil was nothing new to Paul. Having studied the Old Testament, Paul was aware that many people cried out to God for justice (Hab. 1:3, 13). The psalmists shared identical sentiments and called on God to act justly on the wicked (Ps. 7:6; 10:15). For evil to remain unchecked and for injustice to ultimately triumph would call God's righteous character into question. Like the prophets and psalmists, we want our Creator to demonstrate righteousness, to right the wrongs and vindicate the oppressed.

And yet Paul says that God in his forbearance had left sins unpunished. Would God ever demonstrate his justice on sin? Would God ever pour out judgment in such a way that showed both his righteousness and the heinous nature of our wickedness? Paul answers yes—God displayed divine justice at the cross to vindicate his name. At the cross of Jesus, God displayed wrath against sin—the sins of the world that Christ bore.

Jesus is the propitiation for sinners "to show his righteousness at the present time" (Rom. 3:26). While the vindication of God's righteousness will be fully evident on the day of judgment, he has not reserved all judgment for that day. God poured out wrath on the cross to reveal *right now* that he is just. God answered the charges of leaving sins unpunished by sending his Son to the cross.

God planned the death of Jesus "so that he might be just and the justifier of the one who has faith in Jesus" (Rom. 3:26). God is just *and* justifier, the righteous one *and* the one who acquits the guilty. Before the cross, it may not have seemed conceivable that a righteous God could acquit the wicked. But because Jesus bore the wrath of God for the sins of the world, God can now justify sinners who come to Jesus in faith. If Jesus's death on the cross did not quench divine justice on behalf of sinners, God has no basis to justify the wicked.

Reconciled to God by God

Those who trust in Christ are no longer under God's judgment. "There is therefore now no condemnation for those who are in Christ Jesus. For the law of the Spirit of life has set you free in Christ Jesus from the law of sin and death" (Rom. 8:1–2). While there is an end-time judgment for all people, God declares the verdict of justification at the present time for anyone who trusts in Jesus. Believers do not await the final judgment to hear whether God acquits them. "Therefore, since we have been justified by faith, we have peace with God through our Lord Jesus Christ" (Rom. 5:1). We have peace with God *now*. Justification brings reconciliation.

The news of the gospel is that God sent Christ to make a way back to God through his sacrifice. As John Piper puts it, "God himself is the gospel."[7] Believing the gospel should result in exalting God above all things and living for him. Christ died so that God could transform God-belittling and man-centered people into Christ-honoring and glory-beholding people. According to Piper, "If the hearers of the gospel do not see the glory of Christ, the image of God, in all the events and gifts of the gospel, they do not see what finally makes the gospel good news."[8] What is this good news? "God is the final and highest gift that makes the good news good."[9]

The justified have peace and fellowship with God. Their justification by faith is not just a New Testament idea. Paul presents Abraham as an example. "For if Abraham was justified by works, he has something to boast about, but not before God" (Rom. 4:2). To ensure that the object of boasting is God, God justifies the guilty by his grace. Paul quotes Genesis 15:6: "For what does the Scripture say? 'Abraham believed God, and it was counted to him as righteousness'" (Rom. 4:3).

The Bible doesn't say Abraham's faith *was* actual righteousness; rather, "to the one who does not work but believes in him who justifies the ungodly, his faith is counted as righteousness" (Rom. 4:5). On the ledger of Abraham's life, God credited a legal standing of righteousness, and he no longer counted Abraham's sins against him. Paul declares with a psalmist, "'Blessed are those whose lawless deeds are forgiven, and whose sins are covered; blessed is the

---

7. John Piper, *God Is the Gospel: Meditations on God's Love as the Gift of Himself* (Wheaton, IL: Crossway Books, 2005), 17.

8. Ibid., 37.

9. Ibid., 42.

man against whom the Lord will not count his sin'" (Rom. 4:7–8, citing Ps. 32:1–2).

When God reconciles sinners to himself through justification, it means two things: first, God no longer counts sins against the sinner; second, God reckons that sinner's status as righteous. A righteous standing before God is possible because of Christ's work. Jesus "was delivered up for our trespasses and raised for our justification" (Rom. 4:25). Christ's right standing with God makes it certain that any sinner trusting in him will also receive a right standing with God.

The word *imputation* helps explain the transaction between Christ and the sinner: "For our sake he made him to be sin who knew no sin, so that in him we might become the righteousness of God" (2 Cor. 5:21). On the cross, God imputed the sinful status of the world to his Son so that God might then impute the status of righteousness to anyone who trusts in his Son. On the cross, God reckoned Jesus as the perfect sacrifice for sinners. God poured out his wrath on his Son, Jesus propitiated that justice, and now sinners can—in the present—hear God's verdict of "no condemnation" when they trust in this glorious Savior. The cross exalts God as both just and justifier.

Drinking Every Drop of Wrath

One image to explain Jesus's satisfying the wrath of God is the drinking from a cup. This cup has an Old Testament background of outpoured divine wrath. God said, "Take from my hand this cup of the wine of wrath, and make all the nations to whom I send you drink it" (Jer. 25:15). He called his judgment "the cup of his wrath" (Isa. 51:17). God spoke of a day when he could say, "I trampled down the peoples in my anger; I made them drunk in my wrath, and I poured out their lifeblood on the earth" (Isa. 63:6).

In Mark 14, Jesus entered the Garden of Gethsemane and told Peter, James, and John, "My soul is very sorrowful, even to death" (Mark 14:34). What weighed on him was the prospect of God's wrath, for the hour of the cross was nearer than it had ever been. Jesus prayed, "Abba, Father, all things are possible for you. Remove this cup from me. Yet not what I will, but what you will" (Mark 14:36). The Gospels of Matthew, Mark, and Luke all report that in the Garden of Gethsemane, Jesus prayed for the cup to be removed. In Matthew, we learn that Jesus prayed three times for this removal (Matt. 26:39, 42, 44). Yet Jesus committed to the Father's will, and his will was that the Son drink the cup.

The cup was the judgment on sin. Jesus was facing more than crucifixion. He was facing wrath. Many people had been crucified before him and after him, and others would be crucified with him. But Jesus alone would take the cup. He was the seed of the woman promised in Genesis 3:15, and in that verse the victory of God's deliverer would be achieved through personal suffering. Just as God first announced his judgment in a garden, so also in a garden Jesus prepared to endure the judgment of God on behalf of sinners.

Conclusion

When Jesus said "It is finished" (John 19:30), he had drained dry the cup of God's wrath. We deserved judgment, but Jesus took our sins on himself so that, through faith, sinners could be reconciled to God. Michael Horton identifies the good news: "God himself became the Savior. The judge became the deliverer....God's love did not overwhelm or overrule his justice, but fulfilled it. Justice and love, righteousness and mercy, wrath and peace embraced at the cross."[10] The perfect sacrifice of Christ fulfilled the Old Testament system of offerings and became the basis for God's pardon of sinners. The cross demonstrated the righteousness of God. He is just and the justifier of the ungodly. If God has no grounds to acquit the guilty, we are without hope. But Christ Jesus, being truly God and truly man, took the cup of condemnation. Our right standing before God, therefore, is not groundless. Christ is our righteousness.

---

10. Horton, *The Gospel-Driven Life*, 62.

4

GROWTH IN THE GOSPEL

The good news of Jesus is not just for unbelievers. The gospel is for Christians. As we learn to follow Christ, we must not leave behind the gospel in search of deeper messages for growth and maturity. True Christian growth is gospel growth. Daily following Christ means continuing to believe the good news and walking in its light. There is no more profound message than what sinners believe to be saved.

What Believing Is and Isn't

When the gospel is proclaimed, how should we respond? We should repent of our sins and believe in Jesus Christ. But we can't assume a common understanding of what *repent* and *believe* mean.

Not everything that looks like belief in Jesus is actually genuine faith. Believing in Jesus means more than believing he exists. Believing in Jesus is more than acknowledging facts about him. Paul taught that Jesus's death and resurrection fulfilled the scriptures (1 Cor. 15:3–4) and that he proved his resurrection by appearing to various people (1 Cor. 15:5–8). But even the devil believes Jesus died on the cross and rose from the dead. The demons know who Jesus is. A demon-possessed man shouted to him, "What have you to do with me, Jesus, Son of the Most High God?" (Mark 5:7). Another evil spirit cried out, "I know who you are—the Holy One of God" (Luke 4:34). If the demons know Jesus exists and yet are condemned, then their belief is not any God-honoring kind.

Merely knowing the historical facts of the cross and resurrection will not save sinners. Paul says that you must "confess with your mouth that Jesus is Lord and believe in your heart that God raised him from the dead," and then "you will be saved" (Rom. 10:9). Confessing Jesus as Lord echoes Old Testament applications of that title to God. But in Paul's day, there were political overtones to the title "lord" as well. People called the emperor lord. To confess Jesus as Lord meant that Caesar wasn't.

Confessing Jesus as Lord might have cost Christians their lives if the wrong people heard them making such a rival claim. Believing in Jesus meant commitment to him. It was confession even at great cost, signifying allegiance and devotion. True belief led to following him, to discipleship. If you don't think Jesus is calling for radical faith and devotion, reflect carefully on his words: "Whoever loves father or mother more than me is not worthy of me, and whoever loves son or daughter more than me is not worthy of me. And whoever does not take his cross and follow me is not worthy of me" (Matt. 10:37–38).

Jesus is describing what faith looks like. Believing in Jesus means to esteem him above all others, to treasure him above all things, to value him above all earthly relationships. Following Jesus means to love him more than anything else. John Piper explains, "No one is a Christian who does not embrace Jesus gladly as his most valued treasure, and then pursue the fullness of that joy in Christ that honors Him."[1]

However, Christians don't treasure Jesus perfectly. We face temptation to esteem the things of the world above Christ, and many times we may fall headlong into such traps. But the intent of the Christian's heart is different from the unbeliever's heart. The aim of the Christian is to follow Jesus. Demons believe Jesus exists, but they don't follow him and don't want to. The devil knows Jesus died on the cross and rose from the dead, but he doesn't worship him and doesn't want to.

People with genuine belief see Jesus through eyes of faith. They not only see Jesus as the one who died on the cross for their sins and then rose

---

1. John Piper, *Desiring God: Meditations of a Christian Hedonist*, Rev. Ed. (Colorado Springs, CO: Multnomah Publishers, 2003), 54.

victoriously over death, but they see Jesus as glorious, worthy, and majestic, and they worship him. The heart that believes in Jesus follows him. Jesus himself taught, "My sheep hear my voice, and I know them, and they follow me" (John 10:27). The disturbing reality is that many people profess to be Christians but don't follow Jesus. He is not precious to them, they don't esteem him, and they live their lives in an indulgent pursuit of their flesh.

Cheap Grace

We cheapen the gospel when we don't call people to biblical repentance and faith. Dietrich Bonhoeffer said, "Cheap grace is the deadly enemy of our church....The sacraments, the forgiveness of sin, and the consolations of religion are thrown away at cut prices."[2] Cheapening the grace of God compromises the gospel of God. "Cheap grace is grace without discipleship, grace without the cross, grace without Jesus Christ, living and incarnate."[3]

Notice in Matthew 10 that Jesus seemed to make following him *hard*. When times and teachings became tough, Jesus watched many people forsake him during his earthly ministry. When Jesus taught hard truths, "many of his disciples turned back and no longer walked with him" (John 6:66). Those "disciples" were among the larger group of crowd-followers who tracked Jesus's whereabouts with great self-interest. But they couldn't bear some of the things he taught. So they left.

Jesus didn't say, "Wait! Wait! I didn't mean to make it so hard to follow me. Please come back. I can make things easier." Jesus knew such people didn't have true faith. He taught, "If you abide in my word, you are truly my disciples" (John 8:31). Many people appeared to follow Jesus but eventually lost interest. Others claimed faith, but Jesus discerned between true and false faith. Once, after performing miraculous signs in Jerusalem, some people confessed faith in him, but "Jesus on his part did not entrust himself to them, because he knew all people" (John 2:24). Jesus knew that the faith of these people was false. Jesus knew their hearts, and he knows yours.

---

2. Dietrich Bonhoeffer, *The Cost of Discipleship* (New York: Touchstone, 1959), 43.
3. Ibid., 45.

Jesus sees unbelieving hearts in many professing Christians. Jesus knows they're not saved, though they think they are. Why do so many people falsely believe they are Christians? One reason is that believing in Jesus has become formulaic in much of evangelicalism. For example, consider these questions: "Do you believe you're a sinner? Do you believe Jesus died on the cross and rose from the dead? Do you believe Jesus is Lord?" If an unbeliever answers yes to each of these questions, many church leaders and evangelists will pronounce him or her a Christian. But even the demons can answer yes to these questions.

Maybe you're familiar with this format: "Would you repeat this prayer after me? And make sure you're sincere. If you pray this, you'll be saved." After someone voices "the sinner's prayer," the pastor pronounces that person saved: "You've been born again! Welcome to the family of God." Many people think they are Christians when they are no more saved than a parrot who can repeat "the sinner's prayer." When we water down the gospel to trite formulas, we are not helping sinners understand the gospel better. We are muddying the waters by attaching the label *sheep* on goats.

In the New Testament, trusting Jesus is transformative. Following Jesus means turning our values upside down and realigning our lives with the world's true Lord. Trusting Jesus leads to treasuring him. Jesus said, "The kingdom of heaven is like treasure hidden in a field, which a man found and covered up. Then in his joy he goes and sells all that he has and buys that field" (Matt. 13:44). The eyes of faith see Jesus as infinitely valuable and worth any earthly sacrifice. Faith in Jesus is about hoping in him for the sake of who he is—the Savior of sinners, the Pursuer of rebels. Hope in Jesus means looking to him, and nowhere else, for deliverance from God's wrath and the power of sin over us. Seeing Jesus through the eyes of faith means believing that his perfect atonement is sufficient to cover every transgression in our past, present, and future.

The eyes of faith see Jesus as worthy of praise and devotion. Believing in Jesus is about recognizing the value of the King and then worshiping him. If you think you're a Christian because you believe Jesus died on the cross and rose from the dead, you need to ask yourself some questions. *What is my heart's response at the thought of Jesus dying for my sins? What does it mean for Jesus to be my Savior? How has confessing Jesus as Lord transformed my life?* Would you say with Paul, "Indeed, I count everything as loss because of the surpassing worth of knowing Christ Jesus my Lord. For his sake I have suffered the loss of all things and count them as rubbish, in order that I may gain Christ" (Phil. 3:8)? Believing in Jesus involves responding to him and his work with a trust that treasures him and a faith that follows him. Jesus is King.

What Repenting Is and Isn't

Our understanding about Jesus cannot change while our view of sin remains the same. There is no salvation apart from repentance. The word *repentance* means to have a mind change. It is important to understand that repentance begins in the mind because changing behavior can often be mistaken for true repentance. Turning from sin means more than stopping certain behaviors. This is because sin comes "out of the heart" (Matt. 15:19).

There needs to be an internal change, a shift of allegiance from sin to the Savior. Paul meant this when he wrote, "Do not present your members to sin as instruments for unrighteousness, but present yourselves to God as those who have been brought from death to life, and your members to God as instruments for righteousness" (Rom. 6:13).

Sin is not the master of believers, for God has set them free from sin (Rom. 6:14, 18). Repentance is the shifting of allegiance to God from sin. No longer slaves to sin, believers "have become slaves of righteousness" (Rom. 6:18). True repentance results in slavery to righteousness. Repentance, then, is not a turning from sin to nothing in particular; it is turning from unrighteousness to righteousness, from sin to God. Anyone who has died with Christ "has been set free from sin" (Rom. 6:7).

Guilt alone doesn't constitute true repentance. People can feel guilty for sin they never turn from. Paul distinguishes between godly sorrow and worldly sorrow: "For godly grief produces a repentance that leads to salvation without regret, whereas worldly grief produces death" (2 Cor. 7:10).

Some people may feel sorry for their sin because it hurts loved ones, incurs legal consequences, or leads to bouts of self-loathing. Or maybe they just feel sorry they were caught. People may feel sorrow over their sin for reasons that look like repentance but are rooted in selfish motives void of any godly contrition. Paul says that such worldly sorrow leads to death, not salvation.

People can also fear the thought of divine judgment, but this fear doesn't necessarily lead to repentance. Take Felix, the Roman governor of Judea, as an example. As Paul taught him about righteousness, self-control, and coming judgment, Felix was afraid (Acts 24:25). Paul's words evidently struck Felix, who didn't repent but instead dismissed Paul. We cannot frighten people into faith, though the judgment of God should be feared by unbelievers.

Eternal life for sinners is not the result of simply being afraid of hell. True faith and repentance come from hearts that want God because he is God, not from hearts that only fear the consequences of divine wrath. It is possible for sinners to fear judgment for their sin but never have a reverential fear of the Lord. It is possible for sinners to cringe at the notion of hell but shrug at the command for holiness. People can hate the idea of condemnation but never love the God who made them. True repentance begins, then, by acknowledging that our sins have been committed against God.

True repentance also manifests itself in the believer through a transformed view of sin. The believer is to live with a renewed mind, not conforming to the world's sinful patterns any longer (Rom. 12:2). The believer now strives not to sin against God (Ps. 119:11). The believer wants to obey God, to do what is good and pleasing in his sight (Ps. 119:67–68). Rather than seeing God's commands as burdensome and undesirable, the believer meditates on and delights in God's Word (Ps. 119:97–101). Before Christ, the wrong path was desirable; but now, the believer hates the way of disobedience (Ps. 119:104).

Believing and Repenting Sinners

Jesus has imperfect disciples. In fact, there is no other kind. Believers have sinned, and they will sin. In fact, "If we say we have no sin, we deceive ourselves, and the truth is not in us" (1 John 1:8). But the promise is that, "If we confess our sins, he is faithful and just to forgive us our sins and to cleanse us from all unrighteousness" (1 John 1:9). Sinners who have truly repented of sin do not nurture a lifestyle of rebellion against God. However, repentance at conversion doesn't nullify the need for ongoing repentance. Greg Gilbert wrote, "But even if repentance doesn't mean an immediate end to our sinning, it does mean that we will no longer live at peace with our sin. We will declare mortal war against it and dedicate ourselves to resisting it by God's power on every front in our lives."[4]

Christians are repenting sinners. Christians are believing sinners. The evidence of godly sorrow unto salvation is that we continue to be contrite in heart over our sin. David, who was a follower of Yahweh when he wrote Psalm 51, prayed, "Create in me a clean heart, O God, and renew a right spirit within me" (Ps. 51:10). David desired to be pure in heart, to please God through obedience.

Jesus said, "Blessed are the pure in heart, for they shall see God" (Matt. 5:8). Pursuing holiness isn't optional for Christians. Holiness is the idea of following Jesus faithfully, and believers are devoted to Jesus. Turning from sin for the pursuit of holiness is a command: "Strive for peace with everyone, and for the holiness without which no one will see the Lord" (Heb. 12:14). The truly repentant heart is one that desires the path of obedience, a desire not formerly present when the sinner loved the darkness and hated the light.

It's Both or Neither

The words *repent* and *believe* sometimes appear together in the New Testament. When Jesus preached in Galilee, he called people to "repent and believe in the gospel" (Mark 1:15). Paul told the Ephesian elders that he testified to Jews and Greeks "of repentance toward God and of faith in our Lord Jesus Christ" (Acts 20:21).

Sometimes biblical figures commanded repentance without mentioning faith. Jesus said, "Repent, for the kingdom of heaven is at hand" (Matt. 4:17).

---

4. Gilbert, *What Is the Gospel?* 81.

Peter told the crowd at Pentecost, "Repent and be baptized" (Acts 2:38), and he told another crowd, "Repent therefore, and turn again, that your sins may be blotted out" (Acts 3:19). Paul told the Athenians that God "commands all people everywhere to repent" (Acts 17:30).

Other times, biblical figures called for faith in Jesus without mentioning repentance. The narrator of the Gospel of John said that the purpose of recording Jesus's signs was "that you may believe that Jesus is the Christ, the Son of God, and that by believing you may have life in his name" (John 20:31). Peter said that "everyone who believes in him receives forgiveness of sins through his name" (Acts 10:43). Paul told the Philippian jailer, "Believe in the Lord Jesus, and you will be saved" (Acts 16:31). And Paul wrote, "If you confess with your mouth that Jesus is Lord and believe in your heart that God raised him from the dead, you will be saved" (Rom. 10:9).

Though the Bible sometimes speaks of repentance without mentioning faith, and vice versa, it would be a serious mistake to conclude that only one is necessary. Faith and repentance are really two sides of the same coin. Piper says, "One side is tails—turn tail on the fruits of unbelief. The other side is heads—head straight for Jesus and trust His promises."[5] Repentance and faith stand or fall together.

Faith and Repentance as Gifts

In the Bible, God commands people to believe and repent because God is worthy of these things. Yet remember that no one seeks God (Rom. 3:11), no one fears God (Rom. 3:18), the corrupt hearts of sinners are beyond human remedy (Jer. 17:9), and sinners have pledged allegiance to the darkness while hating the light (John 3:19–20). Given these conditions, the fact that anyone repents of sin and believes in Jesus Christ should shock us.

Desiring God is a miracle because true faith and repentance are a work of God's grace. Paul teaches that saving faith is a gift from God: "For by grace you have been saved through faith. And this is not your own doing; it is the gift of God" (Eph. 2:8). Sinners do not innately possess saving faith.

---

5. Piper, *Desiring God*, 64.

When sinners believe in Christ, it has been granted to them (Phil. 1:29). This gracious divine work parallels what Jesus taught. "No one can come to me unless the Father who sent me draws him" (John 6:44), and "no one can come to me unless it is granted him by the Father" (John 6:65).

In John 6, to *come* to Jesus is to *believe* in him, for the phrases "whoever comes to me" and "whoever believes in me" are parallel notions in John 6:35. Jesus taught that sinners are unable to believe in him on their own. If God doesn't grant saving faith, sinners will gladly and willingly remain in their unbelief.

Speaking about repentance, Paul hoped God would grant people "repentance leading to a knowledge of the truth" (2 Tim. 2:25). When Peter announced that Gentiles were turning to Christ and entering the people of God, the Jerusalem church responded, "Then to the Gentiles also God has granted repentance that leads to life" (Acts 11:18). True repentance leads to life, and sinners cannot truly repent on their own. Spiritually blind sinners cannot see the foolishness of their iniquity, and spiritually dead sinners cannot move out of the path of destruction on their own. Piper is right: "We do not make ourselves into Christ-adoring people. We do not muster enough human wisdom or strength or willpower to deliver ourselves from the captivity of Satan's deceits....But in the end, no human means make the miracle of repentance happen."[6]

The reason God must give repentance and faith is to ensure that he remains the object of boasting for salvation. Paul says we have been saved by grace through faith, and that this is a gift of God "so that no one may boast" (Eph. 2:9). If God enables us to do what we could never do on our own (i.e., *believe*), then he alone deserves praise for his saving work.

We must guard against a misunderstanding at this point. God's enabling of our will is not God repenting for us or believing for us. God's enablement doesn't cancel our responsibility or genuine will. When God enables a sinner to believe, that sinner does the believing, and when God grants repentance

---

6. John Piper, *When I Don't Desire God: How to Fight for Joy* (Wheaton, IL: Crossway Books, 2004), 51.

to a sinner, that sinner does the repenting. But because God did the granting, only God deserves the glory. God is glorified, and the sinner is saved.

The Gospel Taking Root

The truly repentant and believing sinner will persevere in repentance and faith because of the miraculous work God has accomplished on the heart that is now alive in Christ. In the ministry of Jesus, he taught that the test of time and trials can expose false confessions. A hard lesson about the kingdom of God is that some people who seem to be believers turn out not to be believers after all.

Have you heard excuses made on behalf of professing Christians who fall away from the faith? "They're just carnal Christians," some say. "Don't worry about them. I remember when they were saved," others insist. "They were brought up right. They'll return after they sow their wild oats," some tell themselves. "I heard them pray the prayer. I saw them baptized," others recall. We must face the tough truth that not every positive response to the gospel is a salvation experience, though many responses appear transformational at first. The test of time can tell tragic tales.

Jesus taught about a farmer sowing seed. Some seeds fell along the path, and birds ate them up. Some seeds fell on rocky places but didn't thrive because of shallow soil, and some fell among thorns that grew up and choked the plants (Mark 4:3–7). This language about seeds was about how people respond to the message of Christ's kingdom. Jesus explained the meaning of the parable. Some people hear the word, but Satan takes away the word that was sown; others receive the message with joy, but trouble and persecution lead them to fall away quickly; and others hear the word but are derailed by the deceitfulness of riches and the worries of this life (Mark 4:14–19). In the parable, we learn that some people confess faith in Jesus without really having faith in Jesus. Saints for a season aren't saints at all. There is no such thing as a temporary Christian.

All hope is not lost. Jesus speaks of the farmer sowing some seed on good soil, and this came up and produced an abundant crop (Mark 4:8).

This depicts people who truly receive the kingdom message with repenting and believing hearts. They hear the gospel, and it goes down deep. In them the gospel takes root.

Root and Fruit

What matters for farmers is that their seed takes root in soil. By analogy, the word of the gospel must grow roots in the receptive sinner or there can be no growth. Jesus specifically said that the seed sown on rocky places had no root (Mark 4:17). But once the seed takes root, it must be allowed to bear fruit that isn't choked by surrounding threats, unlike the seed sown among the thorns of materialism (Mark 4:19). There must be both *root* and *fruit*. Fruit is the proof that something took root in good soil. When preachers sow the gospel, they never know the state of their hearers' hearts. But if God prepares good soil in the heart of a sinner, the word will take root and produce a crop; salvation will happen, and growth will follow.

Believers aren't rootless, and they aren't fruitless. Paul prayed that the Colossians "walk in a manner worthy of the Lord, fully pleasing to him: bearing fruit in every good work and increasing in the knowledge of God" (Col. 1:10). Bearing fruit is part of living worthy of the Lord. So what if someone professes to be a believer yet never bears any fruit? We have to be careful here. The Bible doesn't give us a license to be professional fruit inspectors, but we must not settle for a gospel that says we can have Jesus without any subsequent change. However, we must remember that spiritual growth may look different for different people, such as someone saved out of prison versus someone saved while attending a summer youth camp. The hardened criminal and the young teenager likely have different obstacles before them. Real progress for one might not look like real progress if applied to the other, but only the Lord knows the heart.

Nevertheless, let's emphasize the necessity of bearing fruit. Jesus says, "I am the true vine, and my Father is the vinedresser. Every branch in me that does not bear fruit he takes away, and every branch that does bear fruit he prunes, that it may bear more fruit" (John 15:1–2). Branches without fruit will face destruction: "If anyone does not abide in me he is thrown away like a branch and withers; and the branches are gathered, thrown into the fire, and burned" (John 15:6). The life-giving nourishment of Jesus is not without effect in those who are truly in him. Real connection with Christ brings real change.

Other New Testament writers also emphasize obedience as the demonstration of genuine faith. Paul said that "the fruit of the Spirit is love, joy, peace, patience, kindness, goodness, faithfulness, gentleness, self-control" (Gal. 5:22–23). James said that "faith by itself, if it does not have works, is dead" (James 2:17). Dead faith never saved anyone. Peter commanded his readers to demonstrate the truth of their salvation by bearing the fruit of obedience: "For this very reason, make every effort to supplement your faith with virtue, and virtue with knowledge, and knowledge with self-control, and self-control with steadfastness, and steadfastness with godliness, and godliness with brotherly affection, and brotherly affection with love" (2 Pet. 1:5–7).

These previous verses tell us that when the gospel pierces the heart of a sinner, the gospel grows roots and bears fruit. The warning from John is relevant: "Whoever says 'I know him' but does not keep his commandments is a liar, and the truth is not in him" (1 John 2:4). True Christians follow Jesus, and following him means obeying him and walking in his ways. Following Jesus is the proof of true faith. Genuine repentance and faith will result in a life of repentance and faith. Christians don't believe the gospel for salvation only. The Christian life must be lived in the power of the gospel, or you must call that life something other than Christian.

Commanded to Grow in Christ

Paul commands the Colossians—and, by extension, all Christians—to live centered on Christ: "Therefore, as you received Christ Jesus the Lord, so walk in him, rooted and built up in him and established in the faith, just as you were taught, abounding in thanksgiving" (Col. 2:6–7). The command is to walk in him. The Christian life is walking in Jesus. And Paul connects walking in Jesus with the gospel that the Colossians received when they believed. Knowing the gospel is necessary for salvation and for growth.

The Christian life is lived under the banner of Jesus's lordship. After all, when the Colossians received the truth about Jesus, they received Christ Jesus "the Lord" (Col. 2:6). And that message was to shape their lives. Through the teaching they received from Epaphras, the Colossians were "rooted" in Jesus (Col. 2:7). This image reminds us of Old Testament passages like Psalm 1 where the life of the righteous is rooted in God's Word (see also Jer. 17:7–8). Believers are to be rooted in what they received—the gospel. Paul wants the Colossians—and all Christians—to be "built up" in Jesus (Col. 2:7). We are presently under construction. God's grace, by his Spirit, is building us up in his Son. God is building a fruitful people. Paul wants us to be "established in the faith, just as you were taught" (Col. 2:7). The word *establish* here can mean verify or prove. Christian growth doesn't make God's saving grace effective; it makes God's saving grace evident. This confirmation is what Jesus has in mind when he says that bearing fruit will show people that we are his disciples (John 15:8). Growth in the gospel confirms salvation through the gospel.

When Paul wrote to the believers at Colossae, they were facing a heresy that promised sufficiency, growth, and spirituality outside the gospel of Christ. Paul told them, "See to it that no one takes you captive by philosophy and empty deceit, according to human tradition, according to the elemental spirits of the world, and not according to Christ" (Col. 2:8). Pursuing spiritual growth and experience outside the gospel of Jesus Christ doesn't lead to deeper truth. The spiritual fullness promised by non-gospel messages is hollow and deceptive. The Colossians needed a deeper understanding of the gospel, not a deeper message outside the gospel.

Let's be like the early church. They "devoted themselves to the apostles' teaching" (Acts 2:42). This "teaching" refers primarily to the gospel message about the Savior. As Paul traveled, some of his work involved encouraging believers in their commitment to the gospel, "strengthening the souls of the disciples, encouraging them to continue in the faith, and saying that through many tribulations we must enter the kingdom of God" (Acts 14:22). Paul encouraged the Ephesian elders by saying, "And now I commend you to God and to the word of his grace, which is able to build you up and to give you the inheritance among all those who are sanctified" (Acts 20:32).

Paul wrote to Roman Christians that he was eager to preach the gospel to them (Rom. 1:15). He was eager to preach the gospel to Christians. The gospel is crucial for discipleship, as the Galatians learned when Paul chastised them for turning to a law-centered life after receiving a grace-centered gospel. "I am astonished that you are so quickly deserting him who called you in the grace of Christ and are turning to a different gospel" (Gal. 1:6). Paul refused to set aside God's grace (Gal. 2:21). A grace-formed life shows the power of the cross to both save and sanctify the sinner through the good news.

Conclusion

Unbelievers aren't the only ones who need faith and repentance. The disciple of Jesus pursues a life that honors Jesus, a life that turns from sin and rebellion and trusts Christ's finished work and sufficient grace. Christian growth is not apart from the gospel but in the gospel. When the word of the gospel takes root in sinners, the fruit of obedience confirms the presence of saving faith. The heart that is alive to God is a miracle. By God's grace and for his glory, he grants faith and repentance to sinners so they can hope in Christ as their heart's greatest treasure.

5

PREACHING TO YOURSELF

Since the believer's identity in Christ is a daily reality, the gospel is a daily need. Our souls need to feast on the food of the good news. Through pondering the mercy of Christ that was displayed for sinners on the cross as he became our sufficient substitute, we remind ourselves of his transforming power. We confront our souls with the truth of our deepest identity. "In Christ" is now who we most deeply and truly are.

Saints and Sinners

Every Christian must be a preacher to their own soul. This responsibility is never intended to exclude weekly worship where believers sit in glad submission to the preaching of scripture. Rather, this responsibility is a practice that should be added to the weekly hearing of God's Word on the Lord's Day. You may already hear the gospel once a week, but you need the gospel more than once a week.

The saints are justified sinners. Martin Luther memorably said that Christians are *simul justus et peccator*, or simultaneously righteous and sinful. It will not always be this way—a glory awaits us that will outweigh all our trials and troubles. But for now, God has begun a work in our hearts where warfare rages. Believers face a myriad of temptations that the gospel needs to confront. Believers face envious thoughts, lustful instincts, gossiping words, and feelings of impatience or anger. We face temptations to be bitter, resentful, spiteful, or vengeful. However, our legal standing before God changes from guilty to not guilty, unrighteous to righteous. God sees believers "in

Christ" (Rom. 8:1), and that union with Christ changes our standing before God. Justification is the beginning of a lifelong process during which the Spirit makes the believer more like Jesus Christ.

Paul told the Galatians he was committed to their growth "until Christ is formed in you" (Gal. 4:19). He promised the Philippians that "he who began a good work in you will bring it to completion at the day of Jesus Christ" (Phil. 1:6). Paul also described such transformation with language of glory: "And we all, with unveiled face, beholding the glory of the Lord, are being transformed into the same image from one degree of glory to another" (2 Cor. 3:18).

Ongoing transformation is occurring in the hearts of the saints. In a fallen world, it may be difficult to perceive what is happening to believers. After all, we get sick and die. But inner renewal is happening, day by day (2 Cor. 4:16–17). As saints in a fallen world, we live in imperfect bodies, so part of God's promise to us—and thus part of the Christian hope—is the physical resurrection of our bodies when Christ returns (Rom. 8:23). The Christian's hope is not complete until the Lord returns and raises our corrupted bodies to an incorruptible state (1 Cor. 15:53–54).

In the meantime, we are saints and sinners. We are sinners whom God has set apart for his great purposes. God predestined believers to be conformed to Jesus (Rom. 8:29), a plan that climaxes in glorification (Rom. 8:30). But we live in the tension between the *already* and the *not yet*, between justification and glorification. Sin no longer enslaves the believer (Gal. 5:24), yet we must yield to the Spirit so we don't walk according to the sinful flesh (Gal. 5:16–17). God calls us to live out our new identity in Christ (Rom. 6:2–4). Since we have died with Christ to sin, we must now count ourselves dead to sin and kill the deeds of the flesh (Rom. 6:11; 8:13).

Forgetfulness and Remembrance

We need the gospel every day because, as justified sinners still living in a fallen world, we are prone to forget God rather than remember him. Forgetting God is nothing new, for he warned the Israelites in the Old

Testament about forgetting him (Deut. 6:10–12). God knows the fickle heart of mankind, and he knows that people are prone to wander from him and forget him.

What does it look like to forget God? Moses tells the Israelites, "Take care lest you forget the LORD your God by not keeping his commandments and his rules and his statutes, which I command you today" (Deut. 8:11). Forgetting God means failing to obey him. We face the same danger of forgetting God. He blesses us, yet we disobey him. He delivers us, yet we cherish idols in our hearts.

Moses described God to the Israelites as the one who brought them "out of the land of Egypt, out of the house of slavery" (Deut. 6:12). Israel needed to recall God's past deliverance to not forget him. Yahweh was the God of the Exodus. He pummeled Egypt with plagues and raised up walls of water at the Red Sea. The Israelites needed to keep at the front of their minds the redeeming work of God. If they disobeyed God, they were forgetting the God who rescued them from the hand of Pharaoh. If they forsook God, they were shunning the God who saved them from captivity and destruction.

Israel sang songs to remember their salvation history. Psalms 78, 105, 106, 135, and 136 are examples of how the people recounted God's mighty deeds. Psalm 78 tells of the woes God inflicted on those who forgot what he had done (Ps. 78:11). One such wonder was the Exodus from Egypt, an event of monumental importance to Israel's devotion. Trusting in God meant trusting in the One who delivered them from Pharaoh. God was the one who showed miraculous signs in Egypt (Ps. 78:43), who struck down Egypt's firstborn in the 10th plague (Ps. 78:51), who guided the Israelites safely while engulfing their enemies at the Red Sea (Ps. 78:53). After the Exodus, God led the Israelites with a cloud and fire (Ps. 105:39). They needed food and water, so God fed them and sustained them as they traveled (Ps. 105:41).

Despite these wonders and kindnesses, the people forgot what God had done and put him to the test (Ps. 106:13–14). The fruit of their forgetfulness was disobedience. "They made a calf in Horeb and worshiped a metal image. They exchanged the glory of God for the image of an ox that eats grass. They forgot God, their Savior, who had done great things in Egypt" (Ps. 106:19–21). What haunting words! "They forgot God, their Savior." We need to remember the Lord and his mighty acts. There is no greater act that God has accomplished than the formation of a new covenant through his Son's sacrificial work on the cross.

The cross was God's climactic deliverance of his people, not from Pharaoh but from sin and wrath. The drowning of Pharaoh's armies was a miniscule victory compared to the head-crushing blow of Christ on the serpent's head (Gen. 3:15). When Jesus established the ordinance of the Lord's Supper, he instituted a practice by which believers preach the gospel to one another. During the Last Supper with his disciples, Jesus broke the bread and said, "This is my body, which is for you. Do this in remembrance of me" (1 Cor. 11:24). *Remembrance*—Jesus took the cup and said, "This cup is the new covenant in my blood. Do this, as often as you drink it, in remembrance of me" (1 Cor. 11:25). Again, *remembrance*. Jesus was saying that until he returns, we are to remember the cross—remember what makes the good news good.

Seven Truths to Preach to Yourself

We live out our worldview, and worldviews consist of beliefs. Therefore, it is important for our beliefs to be confronted and shaped by the truths of scripture. As scripture shapes our beliefs, our beliefs restructure our worldview, and our worldview directs our life. There are many truths of scripture we should remember. Let us focus on seven.

First, *God made everyone for his glory*. This is the foundational statement of everything else we say to ourselves. The truth that God made everyone for his glory is why sin is so heinous, it's why we're guilty, it's why God is full of righteous anger, it's why he sent Jesus, and it's why he will judge unbelievers and vindicate his name. Reminding ourselves that everything is about God humbles our proud hearts. God doesn't exist for my purposes; I exist for his. Preaching the gospel to ourselves involves remembering why we are here: to do all things for the glory of God (1 Cor. 10:31). Knowing that we exist for God's glory weakens the pull of worldly enticements for meaning. We were made for the glory of God, not for great riches or world-wide fame or power in the workplace. Because we exist for the glory of God, our highest affections and worship are due to God alone, not to anything or anyone in creation.

Second, *everyone deserves the wrath of God.* We should think about what God has saved us from. Christians should be grateful people since we will not receive what we deserve—God's judgment. God doesn't owe us grace. Every breath and every heartbeat are a gift from him. Christians can be tempted with pettiness. We hold grudges against family members and church members, allow roots of bitterness to grow against parents and spouses, and feel that we have been so offended by this thing or the other that we can never let it go. We need to preach the gospel to ourselves, for our pettiness reveals how easily we forget about the God who has forgiven us of every transgression.

Third, *Jesus died to satisfy God's wrath.* This truth is central to the cross. Redemption for sinners required the wrath-satisfying death of the blameless and righteous Son of God. We were God's enemies, yet he sent Christ to reconcile the world to himself. We did not love him, seek him, or worship him, yet he pursued us with his relentless love while we were rebels and traitors. When believers wonder if God loves them, they must preach to their souls how Christ bore the wrath of God in their place. When Christians battle guilt because of indwelling sin, they must flee to the cross and remember that Christ bore the penalty for every sin—past, present, and future. When saints feel condemned, they must recall that there is no condemnation for all who are in Christ (Rom. 8:1). God has forgiven all sinners who trust in his Son, declaring them justified. As Jerry Bridges says, "To preach the gospel to yourself, then, means that you continually face up to your own sinfulness and then flee to Jesus through faith in His shed blood and righ-teous life. It means that you appropriate, again by faith, the fact that Jesus fully satisfied the law of God, that He is your propitiation, and that God's holy wrath is no longer directed toward you."[1] When we feel unworthy of Christ's sacrifice and wonder how God could ever have forgiven us, we can rest assured that his forgiveness has no basis in us anyway. Clinging to the cross-centered gospel helps us keep our eyes on Christ when our sin causes us to despair.

Fourth, *sin is not the master of the believer*. Christ has not only satisfied sin's penalty, he has broken sin's power (Rom. 6:18). We need to reckon ourselves in line with the reality of our union with Christ. We have died with Christ to sin, so we should count ourselves dead to sin and alive to God (Rom. 6:11). Preach to yourself that by dying with Christ, you have died to sin. Fleeing from sin begins with understanding that the power of the gospel has severed the power of sin. We must remember that sin deceives us and never delivers on its promises. Sin never presents itself honestly. Slavery to sin leads to death (Rom. 6:16). Apart from Christ, sinners embrace what destroys them. Let us call to mind, therefore, the decisive break with sin's power that union with Christ has accomplished. Having died to sin, why should we entertain it, flirt with it, or linger at it? Let our resolve be that of the psalmist who said, "I have stored up your word in my heart, that I might not sin against you" (Ps. 119:11). Burying the gospel deep within us is a strategy to fight against loving and committing sin. The message reminds us that since Christ died for sin, we shouldn't love it. We should not treasure sin, for the essence of sin is to treasure what is not God.

Fifth, *believers are still being saved*. The gospel does not teach salvation as a totally past event. The message of the cross is the power of God "to us who are being saved" (1 Cor. 1:18), indicating an ongoing aspect of salvation. Believers must work out their salvation with fear and trembling (Phil. 2:12–13). God's ongoing work of salvation is called sanctification, which is his grand plan to form a people who reflect the likeness of his Son. Peter told his readers to be holy, for the God who saved them is holy (1 Pet. 1:15). The writer of Hebrews told his readers to "lay aside every

---

1. Jerry Bridges, *The Discipline of Grace: God's Role and Our Role in the Pursuit of Holiness* (Colorado Springs, CO: NavPress, 1994), 59.

weight, and sin which clings so closely, and let us run with endurance the race that is set before us" (Heb. 12:1). It is biblically incoherent to cheapen grace by thinking *I'm forgiven, so now I can live any way I want.* Unbelievers, not believers, want to live in sin. Believers must preach to themselves that the gospel saves them for the purpose of Christlikeness.

Sixth, *suffering serves the sanctification of believers.* The gospel is a cross-centered message, and the cross is also the paradigm for the Christian life (Luke 9:23). The cross was an instrument of torture and death. The pursuit of Jesus is a path marked with suffering along the way. But our suffering is not aimless or purposeless. Through our trials, God is accomplishing things beyond what we can fathom. James teaches that tested faith produces perseverance, and perseverance is part of mature faith (James 1:2–4). God is working all things—not just good things—for our ultimate good (Rom. 8:28). The surpassing value of Christ's kingdom means we should follow Christ no matter the cost. Remember that Jesus called his disciples to radical devotion and discipleship, which he graphically described as taking up an instrument of torture and death. But also preach to yourself that no suffering is ever wasted. Tell your heart to hope with Paul that "the sufferings of this present time are not worth comparing with the glory that is to be revealed to us" (Rom. 8:18).

Seventh, *believers have a sure and incomparable hope.* This truth builds firmly on the last one. God's goal in all things for his people is their good. This hope is both sure and incomparable. It is sure because God never promises beyond what he will deliver. It is incomparable because our glorious future completely transcends all earthly costs paid in this life (2 Cor. 4:17). While we live in a suffering world now—and even suffer ourselves—this will not always be the case. A day of worldwide renewal and transformation is coming, the redemption of all creation, when God will make all things new (Rom. 8:21–22, Rev. 21:5). When the Lord raises the saints and transforms those still alive at his return, we will be fully convinced of truths we now take by faith. The realization of our glorious hope will convince us that every physical pain, every sickness, every emotional turmoil, every mental burden, and every spiritual trial were worth it. God wants the future of his people to affect how they live, so we must tell ourselves what our hope should be. What you hope for will shape how you live. If your hope is anchored in this world only, you will live with a worldly mindset and worldly values. But if your hope is rooted in God's future plan for all things, then you will live with an eternal mindset. We must preach the Christian hope to ourselves so we will live for Christ and not conform to the values of a world passing away.

In Times of Happiness

Circumstances of peace and happiness can, perhaps to our surprise, tempt us to forget God. We can feel so secure that we begin to think and act independently of God. The allure of worldly securities can overshadow their temporary nature. In times of earthly tranquility, we may lose the urgency to be faithful soldiers in a spiritual battle. The blessings of this world can become curses, idols before which we sacrifice what matters most.

God knew that the Israelites would face the temptation of waywardness when he prepared them for entrance into the Promised Land. They would inhabit cities they didn't build, live in houses filled with good things they didn't provide, drink from wells they didn't dig, and glean from vineyards they didn't plant (Deut. 6:10–11). Knowing the blessings in store for the Israelites, God warned them to "take care lest you forget the LORD, who brought you out of the land of Egypt, out of the house of slavery" (Deut. 6:12). The Israelites would be tempted to disobey God in a realm of lavish blessings, so they needed to be aware of who God was, preach to themselves his mighty acts of power, and remember the slavery from which he delivered them.

Maybe you read that warning and think you would never succumb to such a temptation. But overconfidence blinds Christians from the precipice of destruction when they approach it. Using the history of Israel as an illustration, Paul warned the Corinthians, "Therefore let anyone who thinks that he stands take heed lest he fall" (1 Cor. 10:12). We must not presume the security of our current state since we are not above temptation and can easily lose our spiritual footing. Christians may develop an inflated sense of their spirituality, a condition that both blinds and deludes them.

We shouldn't fear blessings or peaceful circumstances. We should, however, keep close watch on our heart's response to them. When Jesus spoke to the rich young ruler, he told him to "sell what you possess and give to the poor, and you will have treasure in heaven; and come, follow me" (Matt. 19:21). But the rich man left sad, "for he had great possessions" (Matt. 19:22). The rich man had treasure but not where it counted. He was blessed with possessions, but he would not give them up for Jesus. Tragically, he treasured his possessions above everything—and everyone—else.

Think back to the parable of the sower in Mark 4. The Word is sown in some people like seed sown among thorns (Mark 4:18). The thorns represent earthly pursuits, and "the cares of the world and the deceitfulness of riches and the desires for other things enter in and choke the word, and it proves unfruitful" (Mark 4:19). We need to preach to ourselves that times of great earthly gain and pleasure have the potential to be spiritually hazardous and destructive.

Paul warned Timothy about the seduction of great wealth: "But those who desire to be rich fall into temptation, into a snare, into many senseless and harmful desires that plunge people into ruin and destruction. For the love of money is a root of all kinds of evils. It is through this craving that some have wandered from the faith and pierced themselves with many pangs" (1 Tim. 6:9–10). When you obsess over income and the possibilities of making more money, preach to yourself the transitory nature and dangerous love of money. Preach to yourself the treasure of Jesus, the one who truly satisfies the soul. Preach to yourself about the slippery surface of self-assurance and pride. Take heed lest you fall.

The wise person builds his or her life on the teaching of Jesus, in good times and in bad. The issue is the quality of the foundation, not the condition of the weather, which changes. Clear skies can quickly fill with storm clouds, and a light breeze can become fierce and deadly. Many professing Christians should reevaluate their foundation. The gospel is not the same thing as the American dream. David Platt says, "We have in many areas blindly and unknowingly embraced values and ideas that are common in our culture but are antithetical to the gospel he [Jesus] taught. Here we stand amid an American dream dominated by self-advancement, self-esteem, and self-sufficiency, by individualism, materialism, and universalism."[2]

We may become so entitled that we think God has wronged us if comforts and luxuries don't materialize at some point. Remember, though, it is hard for the rich to enter the kingdom, and Jesus wasn't just talking about millionaires. On a global scale, when half the world's population live on two dollars per day, *we* are the rich. Platt goes on to say, "The dangerous assumption we unknowingly accept in the American dream is that our greatest asset is our own ability. The American dream prizes what people can accomplish when they believe in themselves and trust in themselves, and we are drawn toward such thinking."[3] Being self-reliant is tricky because seeking moral independence from God was the temptation in Genesis 3:5. We may gain such confidence in ourselves that we reject our need for the gospel.

We always need the gospel, especially when we don't think we need the gospel. When we feel independent of God, we must preach the cross-centered gospel that brings us to our knees and humbles our proud hearts once more. When we feel like abandoning Christian discipleship for the American dream, we must preach to ourselves the message that upholds Jesus as the satisfier of souls. We must preach the gospel to ourselves because our hearts are unreliable and easily deceived. If we don't think we need the gospel when all is well, it's an indication that all is not well.

In Times of Despair

Eugene Peterson says plainly, "A Christian is a person who decides to face and live through suffering. If we do not make that decision, we are endangered

---

2. David Platt, *Radical: Taking Back Your Faith from the American Dream* (Colorado Springs, CO: Multnomah Books, 2010), 19.

3. Ibid., 46.

on every side."[4] Sometimes—many times—we face circumstances that drain our drive and empty our emotions. There may be times when you've cried so much that you can't shed another tear. You may feel that all hope is lost, that there's no light on the horizon, that no one could possibly empathize with your situation. Christians can feel total despair.

I love the book of Psalms for many reasons, particularly because it presents the full array of human emotions. Many psalms portray the writer in hopeless situations, but I think Psalms 42 and 43 are the most helpful in demonstrating the vital practice of preaching to your soul. The psalmist begins by stating his longing for God, a longing that leaves him breathless: "As a deer pants for flowing streams, so pants my soul for you, O God" (Ps. 42:1). The psalmist's desire for God leaves him spiritually thirsty: "My soul thirsts for God, for the living God. When shall I come and appear before God?" (Ps. 42:2).

While the psalmist wants God, he is consumed by personal distress and external taunts. "My tears have been my food day and night, while they say to me all the day long, 'Where is your God?'" (Ps. 42:3). Circumstances were not always miserable. The psalmist recalls times of great joy and celebration: "These things I remember, as I pour out my soul: how I would go with the throng and lead them in procession to the house of God with glad shouts and songs of praise, a multitude keeping festival" (Ps. 42:4). Sometimes remembering the good times—while enduring despairing circumstances—can result in more frustration instead of less.

Then the psalmist models for us what we should do in hopeless situations. He preaches to himself. He asks two synonymous questions: "Why are you cast down, O my soul, and why are you in turmoil within me?" (Ps. 42:5). He then exhorts himself, "Hope in God; for I shall again praise him, my salvation and my God" (Ps. 42:5–6). The psalmist repeats his questions and exhortation two more times (Ps. 42:11; 43:5). Dr. Martyn Lloyd-Jones explains, "The first thing we have to learn is what the Psalmist learned—we

---

4. Eugene H. Peterson, *A Long Obedience in the Same Direction: Discipleship in an Instant Society*, 2nd Ed. (Downers Grove, IL: IVP Books, 2000), 137.

must learn to take ourselves in hand. This man was not content just to lie down and commiserate with himself. He does something about it, he takes himself in hand."[5]

Taking ourselves in hand is not an automatic response. When our soul is in despair, we might consider turning from God and wallowing in self-pity. Instead of being led by his easily deceived heart, the psalmist tells himself what to do. *Hope in God*, he tells his soul. *Hope in God!* Exhorting ourselves about where we should fix our gaze is the remedy to despondency, and we must exhort ourselves again and again and again. Lloyd-Jones adds, "I say that we must talk to ourselves instead of allowing 'ourselves' to talk to us....Am I just trying to be deliberately paradoxical? Far from it. This is the very essence of wisdom in this matter. Have you realized that most of your unhappiness in life is due to the fact that you are listening to yourself instead of talking to yourself?"[6]

Despair has spiritual roots, and preaching the gospel to your soul is an important strategy in this battle. We battle despondency by focusing on God, not on ourselves. We must speak to ourselves about where to fix our hope: *Put your hope in God!* We are stubborn creatures, so firm talk is warranted. Lloyd-Jones also said, "You have to take yourself in hand, you have to address yourself, preach to yourself, question yourself. You must say to your soul: 'Why art thou cast down?'...You must turn on yourself, upbraid yourself, condemn yourself, exhort yourself, and say to yourself: 'Hope thou in God.'"[7]

As the writer of Hebrews said, we must run the race "looking to Jesus, the founder and perfecter of our faith, who for the joy set before him endured the cross, despising the shame, and is seated at the right hand of the throne of God. Consider him who endured from sinners such hostility against himself, so that you may not grow weary or fainthearted" (Heb. 12:2–3). Preaching

---

5. Dr. Martyn Lloyd-Jones, *Spiritual Depression: Its Causes and Its Cure* (Grand Rapids, MI: Wm. B. Eerdmans Publishing Co., 1965), 20.

6. Ibid., 20.

7. Ibid., 21.

the gospel to our downcast souls involves reflecting on the suffering and resolve of Jesus. We must think about the cross. On the cross, Christ bore our shame, our guilt, and our punishment. We must consider Jesus so we will not grow weary and lose heart. We are so weak. Strength in the race comes from meditating on Jesus, not from thinking on something else.

Paul exhorted the believers similarly:

> *So we do not lose heart. Though our outer self is wasting away, our inner self is being renewed day by day. For this light momentary affliction is preparing for us an eternal weight of glory beyond all comparison, as we look not to the things that are seen but to the things that are unseen. For the things that are seen are transient, but the things that are unseen are eternal.*

—2 Cor. 4:16–18

Fix your eyes, your soul, on Christ. Preach the gospel of Christ's lordship to your downcast soul. Despair for the believer is temporary. A day is coming when God will wipe every tear (Rev. 21:4).

Conclusion

With condemnation behind us and glory before us, we have hearts in daily need of good news. The hardness of life leaves us weak, and the toll of suffering leaves us vulnerable. In times of happiness and despair, our souls need to feast on the gospel of the Lord Jesus Christ. We must speak truth to our hearts because the Bible warns about forgetting the Lord. We preach to our souls so we can cultivate a certain mindset. Hopeless situations don't inevitably lead to a downcast soul, but they can. You must be ready, armed with the gospel. According to Piper, "Hearing the word of the cross, and preaching it to ourselves, is the central strategy for sinners in the fight for joy. Nothing works without this. Here is where we start. And here is where we stay. We never outgrow the gospel."[8]

---

8. Piper, *When I Don't Desire God*, 91.

6
LOVING WHAT JESUS LOVES

We should not hate anything that Jesus loves, and he loves the church. When God saves sinners through the gospel, they become part of the church of Jesus Christ. But many professing Christians want nothing to do with his people. Do you love what Jesus loves? The New Testament has no category for following Jesus disconnected from the gathered assembly of the saints. Devotion to Jesus includes devotion to his people.

The Bride of Jesus

The question "What is the church of Jesus?" has more than one right answer. In the New Testament, the church is the bride of Christ. Suppose someone approached you and said, "I hate your wife. She's ugly, and I want nothing to do with her. But you and I can be friends." How would you respond? That's an awkward way to begin a relationship with anyone. But many professing Christians say, "Jesus, I want you. But I hate your church. She's ugly, and I want nothing to do with her."

When professing Christians berate the church of Christ, they are berating the bride of Christ. According to John 3:29, "The one who has the bride is the bridegroom. The friend of the bridegroom, who stands and hears him, rejoices greatly at the bridegroom's voice. Therefore this joy of mine is now complete." John the Baptist, who spoke those words, was the friend of Jesus, the bridegroom. John was full of joy at the arrival of Jesus, for he had come for his people, the bride. A wedding was a time for celebration.

The New Testament has at least three truths to teach us about the church as the bride of Christ. First, Jesus died for his bride. If Jesus died for the church, then we should not disparage what Jesus purchased with his blood. Paul used Jesus's sacrificial death for the church as his analogy for how husbands should love their wives. "Husbands, love your wives, as Christ loved the church and gave himself up for her" (Eph. 5:25). The words *gave himself up* refer to the voluntary humiliation of his crucifixion. No one took his life from him; he gave it up (John 10:18). And he didn't give his life up for something abstract—he died for the church. When Paul warned the Corinthians against causing the weak among them to stumble, he said, "And so by your knowledge this weak person is destroyed, the brother for whom Christ died" (1 Cor. 8:11). The church is the blood-bought bride of Jesus (Acts 20:28).

Second, Jesus cares for his bride. Paul said, "In the same way husbands should love their wives as their own bodies. He who loves his wife loves himself. For no one ever hated his own flesh, but nourishes and cherishes it, just as Christ does the church" (Eph. 5:28–29). Jesus shows his love for the church by caring for and strengthening it. Jesus cleanses the church with his gospel word (John 15:3). He nourishes his people so they may grow and bear fruit (John 15:4–5). Jesus never forsakes his people, and nothing can separate us from God's love in Christ. Apart from Jesus, the church cannot love and live for him.

Third, Jesus is returning for his bride. The first stage of a Jewish wedding was the engagement, and that's the period of time in which Christians live. We have been promised to one husband, Christ (2 Cor. 11:2), a betrothal sealed at conversion. Just as there would be a presentation of the bride to the bridegroom on the wedding day, a day of presentation will also occur for the church. Jesus will "present the church to himself in splendor, without spot or wrinkle or any such thing, that she might be holy and without blemish" (Eph. 5:27). This presentation of the church to Christ will occur at his triumphant return. The wedding day will be one of glorification and transformation. Even now the church is a beautiful bride, justified by the grace of God and clothed in the righteousness of Christ alone. Jesus is a faithful bridegroom who will never leave her for another.

The Body of Jesus

Salvation has both individual and corporate aspects, and marginalizing either aspect results in an inadequate understanding of what God does when he saves sinners. God redeems sinners individually, but at conversion, believers are also "baptized into one body—Jews or Greeks, slaves or free—and all were made to drink of one Spirit" (1 Cor. 12:13). Having thought about the church as the bride of Jesus, now we need to think about it as the body of Jesus.

First, a body has a head. Jesus is the head of his body, the church (Col. 1:18). Neither a church's pastor nor any of its members is the head of Christ's church. As head, Jesus is the church's authoritative guide and Lord, source and nourishment. Jesus is the great Shepherd of his sheep (Heb. 13:20). Bridal language overlaps with body language in Ephesians: "For the husband is the head of the wife even as Christ is the head of the church, his body, and is himself its Savior" (Eph. 5:23). Paul then notes that "the church submits to Christ" (Eph. 5:24), which is the appropriate response of the body to its head. Proper body function means that the members of the body obey the head. If the head wants the feet to move and they won't, something is wrong with the organic connection between the head and the body.

Second, a body has members. "For just as the body is one and has many members, and all the members of the body, though many, are one body, so it is with Christ" (1 Cor. 12:12). Individual believers are the parts of Christ's body. Paul taught that the composition of the members is ethnically diverse—"Jews or Greeks"—and socially inclusive—"slave or free," for "all were made to drink of one Spirit" (1 Cor. 12:13). Racism has no place in the body of Christ, for all people in Christ drink from the same Holy Spirit. While categories of social status matter to the world, believers must see people differently through the eyes of Christ.

Third, a body needs all its members. As justified sinners, we may face the temptation to feel inferior to others. We must preach to ourselves that all believers belong to the church. "If the foot should say, 'Because I am not a hand, I do not belong to the body,' that would not make it any less a part of the body. And if the ear should say, 'Because I am not an eye, I do not belong to the body,' that would not make it any less a part of the body" (1 Cor. 12:15–16). On the other hand, sometimes we must confront attitudes of superiority in the church. "The eye cannot say to the hand, 'I have no need of you,' nor again the head to the feet, 'I have no need of you'" (1 Cor. 12:21). The parts of the body—the members of the church—need one another. God designed his church "that there may be no division in the body, but that the members may have the same care for one another" (1 Cor. 12:25).

Fourth, a body has various abilities. Eyes can see, ears can hear, feet can walk, hands can hold, mouths can speak. These functions are analogous to the fact that the Holy Spirit has given each believer at least one spiritual gift for the edification of the body (1 Cor. 12:7). "For as in one body we have many members, and the members do not all have the same function, so we, though many, are one body in Christ, and individually members of one another" (Rom. 12:4–5). Lists of spiritual gifts appear in Paul's and Peter's letters (Rom. 12:6–8; 1 Cor. 12:8–10; Eph. 4:11; 1 Pet. 4:10–11), but none of the lists is exhaustive. Each believer is responsible to serve and edify the body of Christ with spiritual gifts. As Peter says, "As each has received a gift, use it to serve one another, as good stewards of God's varied grace" (1 Pet. 4:10). The Holy Spirit sovereignly distributes spiritual gifts to the people of God (1 Cor. 12:11).

Fifth, a body is concerned about all its members, not just some of them. There are times when one part of the body affects other parts. A throbbing head can make your stomach sick; overworking your arms can strain your back; spraining an ankle can make your whole foot hurt. Paul wrote about the connection believers have with one another in the body of Christ: "If one member suffers, all suffer together; if one member is honored, all rejoice together" (1 Cor. 12:26). The parts of the body should "have the same care for one another" (1 Cor. 12:25). The body of Christ is the place for Christian love and care to be displayed and cultivated. A local church may consist of people who are different from us, yet God's sovereign and varied grace has designed diversity for the good of his people and the glory of his name.

A Low Priority

Many professing Christians have a low view of the church's value, a tragedy that means there is much confusion about the Christian faith. There is misunderstanding about what God expects from his people. He wants a gathered people sharing life together and loving one another. He wants people serving, giving, and sacrificing. He wants people to love, compromise, and edify each other. He wants people to worship God, evangelize unbelievers, and disciple the nations. Jesus wants the church to be the church.

Yet many attenders are completely disengaged from the life of the church body. I resonate with this lament from Eugene Peterson: "One of the afflictions of pastoral work has been to listen, with a straight face, to all the reasons people give for not going to church....I listen (with a straight face) and go home and pray that person will one day find the one sufficient reason for going to church, which is God."[1] There are at least six common reasons people give for why they don't attend church or, if they do attend, why they don't pursue church involvement.

First, "Sunday is the only time I have with my family." If Sunday is a day off work, people want those precious hours at home instead of at church. But let's look at the situation differently. If the only time you have with your family is on Sunday, then for the sake of their souls and yours, take them to worship with the people of God that day. What better time as a family could you pursue than worshiping together under the Word of God? If you don't guide your family into weekly worship with God's people, think about what you are communicating to your children about God. You're saying that alternative activities are more important than participating in the corporate worship of God.

---

1. Peterson, *A Long Obedience in the Same Direction*, 49.

Second, "We're just too busy." If you're too busy to be connected to a local church, you're too busy. When something is really important to us, we prioritize it. The excuse of busyness is an admission about church as a low priority. We all have the same number of hours in a week. And if we make time for things that don't matter, thus displacing time for what matters most, we're not doing what is best for ourselves or our families. Many good things vie for our devotion, but the church of Jesus Christ is the best choice. Before you can teach your children what matters most, you must first make sure it matters most to you. We will live out what matters to us, and our children will see it. The gospel must wreck our worldly priorities and shatter our worldly delusions. We must have our minds sobered by what is worth living and dying for. If what matters to you is growing in the gospel and helping others do the same, then you will not marginalize the church of Jesus Christ.

Third, "I attended when I was a kid." Devotion to Christ's church is not something we age out of. Adults who give this excuse reveal a misunderstanding of why Christians attend corporate worship in the first place. Maybe as a kid this person found church boring, unengaging, and irrelevant. What's necessary, then, is explanation about why and how God engages his people in the worship assembly, why preaching is crucial for the growth of the believer, and why serving in a local church is an act of obedience to God. If someone attended church only when they were young, perhaps they never understood or believed the gospel. Perhaps they never grasped the value of the bride and body of Christ. It's not too late.

Fourth, "There are too many hypocrites in the church." A hypocrite is someone who claims to be something they're not. However, most Christians don't claim to be perfect. When most people complain about hypocrites in the church, they mean something like, "This person claims to be a Christian but does things that are unchristian." Yes, Christians sin, but they are repentant sinners, justified by grace through faith. Christians have an advocate, Christ, who dispels the accusations of the evil one. The Bible doesn't assure us that Christians will never do something ungodly. The church is full of broken people who don't have it all together, sinners who need grace and cling to Christ as their only hope.

Fifth, "Going to church doesn't make you a Christian." Attending church doesn't save a sinner, but it is where the saved should gather. Christians care about obeying the Lord, and part of obedience includes gathering with God's people (Heb. 10:24–25). This excuse exposes a fundamental me-centered attitude. To be a God-centered disciple, you need the church of Jesus Christ. It takes a church to make a faithful Christian. Charles Spurgeon spoke clearly and strongly about Christians giving themselves to the church:

> I know there are some who say, "Well, I hope I have given myself to the Lord, but I do not intend to give myself to any church, because "Now why not?" Because I can be a Christian without it." Now, are you quite clear about that? You can be as good a Christian by disobedience to your Lord's commands as by being obedient?...There is a brick—a very good one. What is the brick made for? To help to build a house with. It is of no use for that brick to tell you that it is just as good a brick while it is kicking about on the ground as it would be in the house. It is a good-for-nothing brick; until it is built into the wall, it is no good. So you rolling-stone Christians, I do not believe that you are answering your purpose; you are living contrary to the life which Christ would have you live, and you are much to blame for the injury you do.[2]

Sixth, "Church is boring." Amusement is a terrible reason to judge the value of something, and because amusement is subjective, this excuse also reveals a me-centered mindset. We should worship corporately because we want to worship God with his people, hear from his Word, and edify the body with our spiritual gifts. A normal church service may not sound spectacular. But things are not what they seem. Gather with God's people prayerfully, expectantly. Sing loudly and with conviction. Receive the sermon like the Thessalonians received Paul's instruction—as the very word of God (1 Thess. 2:13). God's word doesn't return void.

---

2. Charles H. Spurgeon, *The Complete Works of C. H. Spurgeon, Volume 60: Sermons 3387 to 3439* (Delmarva Publications, 2013), Google Books.

Why the Church Matters

Since the church matters to Jesus, it should matter to you. Having discussed some excuses people give for not gathering together with a church, let's examine the biblical foundation for the church's significance. There are at least three biblical reasons why Christians should worship corporately.

First, Christians have a mandate to gather. This means that involvement in the body of Christ is obedience to Christ, "not neglecting to meet together, as is the habit of some, but encouraging one another, and all the more as you see the Day drawing near" (Heb. 10:25). The assembly of the saints is assumed throughout the New Testament. The authors of the letters addressed their writings to churches and to people who worked in churches. No New Testament writer conceives of churchless disciples of Jesus. When you followed Jesus, you followed him with a band of brothers and sisters in the body of Christ. In fact, it is impossible to obey certain biblical commands without involvement in church. How can you be devoted to one another in love (Rom. 12:10) if you aren't gathering with the saints? How can you exercise church discipline against wayward and unrepentant members (1 Cor. 5:1–13) if you don't belong to a church body that prioritizes church health? How can you build up the body of Christ with your spiritual gifts (1 Cor. 12:7) if you don't attend a church where you can serve? Gathering with other believers is what makes obedience to other commands possible, commands you would disobey if you refused to fellowship with the people of God. Christians should ultimately worship with the saints because they want to obey God. "Churchless Christianity makes about as much sense as a Christless church, and has just as much biblical warrant."[3]

Second, Christians have a message to protect. God has entrusted the gospel of Jesus Christ to the people of God. Believers should gather together because they share the hopeful message of Christ crucified and risen. Jude wrote to believers who were surrounded by false teachers: "Beloved, although I was very eager to write to you about our common salvation, I found it

---

3. Kevin DeYoung and Ted Kluck, *Why We Love the Church: In Praise of Institutions and Organized Religion* (Chicago: Moody Publishers, 2009), 164.

necessary to write appealing to you to contend for the faith that was once for all delivered to the saints" (Jude 1:3). The saints must guard the gospel. When we gather together, we reaffirm the truths we hold dear. We preach the Word so believers will receive correction, rebuke, and encouragement (2 Tim. 4:2). We must resist erroneous teachings that undermine the truth about Jesus Christ (Gal. 1:6–7). We must be discerning against hollow and deceptive human philosophies (Col. 2:8). Churches, especially the leadership (Titus 1:9), must guard the gospel against distortion from without and from within the body. Are you doing your part to protect the gospel message by your corporate presence and affirmation of sound doctrine? Are you seeking to uphold the true gospel of Jesus by singing it, praying it, and hearing it proclaimed with the saints to whom God entrusted it?

Third, Christians have a mission to go. Jesus commissioned the church, "Go therefore and make disciples of all nations, baptizing them in the name of the Father and of the Son and of the Holy Spirit, teaching them to observe all that I have commanded you. And behold, I am with you always, to the end of the age" (Matt. 28:19–20). No one else is taking a message of salvation to the nations. Only the church of Jesus Christ proclaims the message that saves sinners from God's wrath in an eternal hell. Only Christians herald this news. So if God hasn't commissioned anyone other than the body of Christ to spread the good news about Jesus, how will the nations hear if we are disobedient? And how will we be obedient to the Great Commission if we don't care enough about the body of Christ to worship corporately and be involved with other believers? God's Spirit empowers their witness to the nations.

The Need for Humility

Like any close family, the church inevitably has conflicts. The question isn't whether church members will have problems with one another; the question is whether church members will handle conflict in Christ-honoring ways. Too often, conflict provokes more acts of the flesh than the fruit of the Spirit. The gospel is for church members, too. The commands about believers relating with others drip with gospel language. I want to examine four areas in which the gospel should impact how Christians relate to one another in church life—humility, forgiveness, love, and peace.

The gospel should affect how we think about other believers. In Philippians 2, Paul presents the example of Christ's incarnation and crucifixion to portray the appropriate attitude of believers toward one another. "Have this mind among yourselves, which is yours in Christ Jesus" (Phil. 2:5). It all starts in the mind. If the gospel isn't affecting our thinking, we may be fooling ourselves and others about what the Lord is doing in us. One of the ways our thinking should be affected is in our attitudes toward other Christians. Paul wrote, "Do nothing from selfish ambition or conceit, but in humility count others more significant than yourselves" (Phil. 2:3). Humility asks, *How can I serve others?* instead of *How can others serve me?* Humility doesn't call for a total disregard of self. While your interests aren't unimportant, they're not most important. We should be willing to lay aside our agendas for the sake of our brothers and sisters in Christ.

There are professing Christians who wreak havoc on congregations because they will never set aside their personal preferences. Their way is the right way, and they intend to get their way no matter the cost. They're not concerned with the unchristian nature of their actions, nor do they care who they hurt. Their concern is being right, not being righteous. Church members should pray for humility toward other believers, for this was the attitude of Jesus. He "emptied himself, by taking the form of a servant, being born in the likeness of men. And being found in human form, he humbled himself by becoming obedient to the point of death, even death on a cross" (Phil. 2:7–8). Rather than seeking their own interests in church settings, believers should strive to serve and lift up one another.

Humble attitudes defuse unhealthy church conflict. I say *unhealthy* conflict because some conflict is necessary, like the defense of core doctrines in the faith. If leaders in the church teach that Jesus isn't the only way for sinners to be saved, then believers should proclaim the Christ-alone gospel and oppose such false teachers. If the preacher describes the Bible as a human book with no greater authority than other literature, then believers should insist that God's inspired Word is the final authority in matters of faith and practice.

But most church conflict isn't about pluralism or the nature of the Bible. Most squabbling occurs over minor things that have no eternal value. Churches fight over musical styles, the election of leaders, the allotment of funds, paint and carpet colors, stained glass windows, and other matters unrelated to the message of the gospel. Church members squabble over how many songs to sing, who plays the piano, when choir practice begins and ends, and the length of the pastor's sermon. The solution to such bickering is the gospel—a message about the crucified Messiah who came in humility and gave his life for others.

Humility in the body of Christ is about obedience or disobedience. Paul told his readers to "walk in a manner worthy of the calling to which you have been called, with all humility" (Eph. 4:1–2). We can't think about fellow believers any way we want and assume it doesn't matter. It matters. God doesn't want us to withdraw from church life simply because we encounter stubborn people with selfish ambitions. How can we obey the command to be humble if we follow the trajectory of our wounded pride and leave? If we leave a church because it contains stubborn and selfish people, we will go to another church only to find stubborn and selfish people. We are sinners sharing life with other sinners.

Consider that God sanctifies us through relationships with difficult people. Paul gave this personal testimony about a thorn in his flesh, a messenger of Satan given to display the sufficiency of Christ's grace in Paul's weakness (2 Cor. 12:7–9). We need difficult people. It's good to be in a church where people prefer different things than we do, and it's good to be in a church where our preferences aren't always accommodated. The crux is whether we're learning the lesson of Christ's sufficient grace or whether we're becoming bitter against God and our Christian family.

A thorn in our flesh is a sign of God's grace to us. Humility doesn't come without wounds. How will we ever learn to be humble toward others if nothing and no one requires humility from us? Dependence on God's grace is the beginning of humility. We learn humility by serving others, especially those who challenge our patience and compassion.

An attitude of humility can defuse tensions between feuding individuals. If your enemy is hungry or thirsty, offer food and drink (Prov. 25:21–22). Jesus told his followers to love their enemies and pray for those who persecuted them (Matt. 5:44). If the only people you treat well are those who treat you well, you're not following the example of Jesus. Even unbelievers return kindness for kindness (Matt. 5:46).

We must seek to cultivate an attitude of humility by preaching the gospel to ourselves. There's nothing like the message of the cross to humble sinners; apart from Christ, we have no source of salvation. We don't deserve grace, yet Jesus humbled himself unto an obedient death on the cross. An attitude of humility toward others isn't based on whether we think they deserve it. Who of us deserved the humble sacrifice of Jesus?

The Need for Forgiveness

"Every one says forgiveness is a lovely idea," C. S. Lewis wrote, "until they have something to forgive."[4] Paul wanted his readers to be "bearing with one another and, if one has a complaint against another, forgiving each other; as the Lord has forgiven you, so you also must forgive" (Col. 3:13). This verse assumes that believers will need to grant forgiveness to other believers. We will sin against one another. But thinking about God's forgiveness of us is key to understanding our forgiveness of others.

If you withhold forgiveness from believers, you are disobeying God's command to forbear with them (Eph. 4:2). If someone sins against you, you should go to that person and talk about it instead of talking to others about it. "If your brother sins against you, go and tell him his fault, between you and him alone" (Matt. 18:15). It is important to address the issue between

---

4. Lewis, *Mere Christianity*, 104.

the two of you so slander doesn't start. Paul tells believers to rid themselves of malice and slander (Col. 3:8), and we need to preach this to ourselves when another believer sins against us.

The deeper you move into serving the body of Christ and the more responsibility you share in ministry areas, the greater the potential for a wounded heart. Though such a possibility shouldn't stop you from serving, it will keep you from being surprised when the words and actions of others cause you to reevaluate why you do what you do. You won't always feel appreciated; you may be taken for granted, and you might feel like someone else would do a better job. We can't minister for the sake of pleasing people because we'll never please everybody. We should serve the church because Christ has saved us, not because we receive the approval of people.

You've likely spotted others' faults and quirks, but you have them, too, and others have noticed. You should extend forgiveness to others who wrong you because one day you will need forgiveness for wronging others. Serving the church sanctifies the saints because serving with other sinners reveals how unchristian we can behave. We may not realize how selfish we are, how belligerent we can be, or how difficult we are to work with, until others point it out. There is wisdom in accepting the correction of others (Prov. 11:2; 12:1).

When you're sinned against, you should forgive "as the Lord has forgiven you" (Col. 3:13). When we find forgiveness difficult, and we will, we should reflect on how the Lord has forgiven us. When the sins of others anger us, we should think about how our sin once provoked God's holy wrath. We must preach the gospel to ourselves. We must think about propitiation and justification, how Christ's righteousness is the basis for our standing with God, and how that standing is possible because Christ satisfied God's wrath so he could pardon sinners. "Blessed is the man against whom the LORD counts no iniquity, and in whose spirit there is no deceit" (Ps. 32:2).

Since God has pardoned us, who are we to withhold forgiveness from fellow believers? Would we insist that we have reason to be bitter against others when God, who is almighty and holy, has canceled the debt of sin against us? Jesus told a parable about an unmerciful servant whose outstanding debts were canceled by his master (Matt. 18:23–27). The servant then went to a fellow servant and said, "Pay what you owe" (Matt. 18:28). When the master found out what happened, he summoned the unmerciful servant into his presence and said, "And should not you have had mercy on your fellow servant, as I had mercy on you?" (Matt. 18:33). We should forgive someone of their sins against us since God has canceled our countless transgressions for which we deserved his eternal wrath. A repenting sinner must be a forgiving sinner because a repenting sinner is a forgiven sinner. Here's what Greg Gilbert says:

> I wonder if your understanding of the gospel of Jesus Christ—the good news that Jesus saved you even though you didn't deserve it—is deep enough to swallow up the little criticisms you have of your brothers and sisters. I wonder if it's deep enough to sink the offenses they've committed against you, even the most painful ones, and lead you to forgive them and love them just as Jesus himself has done for both of you.[5]

The Need for Love

After speaking about forgiveness, Paul tells the Colossians, "And above all these put on love, which binds everything together in perfect harmony" (Col. 3:14). The greatest commandment is to love God, and the second is to love your neighbor (Matt. 22:36–40). Love fulfills the law (Rom. 13:10) and is the first fruit of the Spirit that Paul lists (Gal. 5:22). A guiding question for Christian behavior should be *Am I loving this person by what I am saying or doing?*

Perhaps no one is as strong and clear on the subject of Christians loving one another as John, evident in his Gospel and in his first epistle. "A new commandment I give to you," Jesus said, "that you love one another: just as I have loved you, you also are to love one another" (John 13:34). Jesus's words are powerful because they appeal to his own act of love as the example

---

5. Gilbert, *What Is the Gospel?* 118.

for others to follow. As the Lord forgave, we should forgive. And as the Lord loved, we should love.

Love for others is a confirmation of faith. Jesus said, "By this all people will know that you are my disciples, if you have love for one another" (John 13:35). If someone claims to love God yet hates God's people, John calls that person a liar (1 John 4:20–21). If you are struggling with loving the body of Christ, preach to yourself that we love because God first loved us (1 John 4:19). When Jesus went to the cross, we were his enemies, condemned under wrath (Rom. 5:8–10). When Jesus died for us, we were not seeking God, our words and actions were wicked, and we had no fear of God (Rom. 3:11–18). When Jesus died on the cross to demonstrate his love for us, he purchased atonement for our hatred of him when we were dead in our transgressions.

Some people may seem unlovable, but think about how unworthy you are of God's great love and kindness shown in Christ. Contemplate your unrighteousness. Ponder the reality that God loved you first. There we were, objects of wrath, yet God set his great love and mercy on us and made us alive (Eph. 2:3–5). By God's grace and the power of his Spirit, you can love those who seem unlovable. You can embrace with genuine kindness and compassion the members of the body of Christ who have hurt you or hurt those close to you. You can love them because Jesus loved you.

The Need for Peace

God calls Christians to let peace rule in their hearts (Col. 3:15). The people of God must be united. Paul wanted his readers to be "eager to maintain the unity of the Spirit in the bond of peace" (Eph. 4:3). A church dishonors God if they divide over non-gospel issues. Paul told the Corinthians, "I appeal to you, brothers, by the name of our Lord Jesus Christ, that all of you agree, and that there be no divisions among you, but that you be united in the same mind and the same judgment" (1 Cor. 1:10). Church members must not sacrifice peace and unity for the sake of their personal agendas.

To cultivate a mindset of pursuing peace in the church, Christians should preach to themselves the gospel that announces their peace with God. Since we have been justified through faith, we have peace with God (Rom. 5:1). Apart from Christ there was only condemnation, but there is no condemnation for all who are in Christ (Rom. 8:1). God made peace with sinners through the blood of his Son (Col. 1:20), and now that peace should manifest in church relationships. In other words, if believers are at peace with God, they should be at peace with one another.

Determining to have your way on non-gospel issues isn't worth disunity in the church. Paul reserves strong words for those who damage churches: "If anyone destroys God's temple, God will destroy him. For God's temple is holy, and you are that temple" (1 Cor. 3:17). The church of Jesus is a people, not a place. But I have attended church business meetings where materials in the building seemed to matter more than the people who worship there. Our buildings can become idols when elevated over loving our fellow believers and considering them better than ourselves. If you saw someone poking himself in the eye or sawing off his foot, you'd assume something was seriously wrong. God sees feuding church members this way.

Are you making every effort to keep the unity of the Spirit in the bond of peace? When you are dealing with non-gospel issues in the church, you should ask, *How will this affect unity in the body of Christ? Will this keep peace among us, or will it divide us?* A divided church engages in divided worship, and God is not pleased. Worship is the primary purpose of gathering as the people of God. If a church cannot worship together, how can anyone take anything else they do seriously?

When faced with disunity in the church, we should preach the gospel of God's peace to our souls. God reconciled us to himself, making peace through Christ's blood so we might be united with—not divided from—the saints. We should treat the body of Christ with care and love, knowing that Christ died for our brothers and sisters (1 Cor. 8:11). It is the appropriation of the gospel that cultivates the essential attitudes of humility, love, forgiveness, and peace.

Conclusion

From the foundation of the world, God has loved his people. And when he awakens sinners by his Spirit, he is building his church. Gathering with the people of God for worship is a testimony to God's redeeming work in our hearts. We are a people made by mercy, and our devotion to God includes a devotion to Christ's church. The church of Christ is called to be a gospel-guarding, gospel-heralding people. There may be reasons why professing Christians view church as a low priority, but the Bible's emphasis on the gathering of God's people should cause us to reevaluate what matters to us. Jesus loves the church, and so should we. The local assembly of the saints is the realm where we pursue love, forgiveness, humility, and peace with one another. It is where we gather with those who are different from us, where those differences display the tapestry of saving grace.

7
BUILDING THE BODY

The way churches grow is not a secret. Ministers and members should want their church to be healthy, and healthy church growth is shaped and empowered by the gospel. Church leaders, in particular, need discernment on this subject because we live in a culture where more is better, efficiency is ideal, boredom is the enemy, amusement is expected, cool is crucial, and edgy is effective. The worldly values of the culture have had a devastating effect on many churches.

When the Gospel Becomes a Product

Commercials tell us what is the latest and greatest in the world of technology. But the moment you buy a new form of technology, someone is already developing something better. It's impossible to keep up with the innovation game. Businesses need more and more consumers, so they're always trying to reinvent themselves, present what they make in more appealing ways, or compensate for previous inadequacies in their products.

When it comes to church ministry, we shouldn't try to reinvent the wheel, yet that is exactly what many leaders are trying to do. If the church is a business, and every business has a product to sell, then the product of the church is the gospel. The problem, though, is that unregenerate people are offended by the true gospel. Jews stumble over it, and Gentiles think it's stupid (1 Cor. 1:18). But a business mentality will not settle for failure. To get people to buy the church's product, some churches believe you have to do one of two things.

First, you may have to alter the gospel. If you're in the business of pushing a product and people aren't buying that product, you must improve the product or the business closes its doors. Maybe people will purchase the gospel if you tell them Jesus wants to be their friend, their buddy. Try telling them that Jesus wants them to be healthy and wealthy. Tell them that Jesus wants to make their great life even better. He wants to give them bigger homes, higher-paying jobs, nicer friends, more obedient children, yards without weeds, parking spots near the front. To really reel them in, tell them that following Jesus is easy and that all they need to do is believe a few simple things. Keep it simple. Don't complicate it too much or they'll second-guess their interest in your product and go somewhere else. Close the sale or lose the buyer.

Second, you may need to distract the buyers with something—a gimmick. Emphasize aspects of the church that are amusing and comfortable. Tell about all the programs. Make clear how nonjudgmental everyone is. Fresh coffee? You've got it. Comfortable seating? You've got that, too. Casual, laid-back atmosphere? Absolutely! The impulse to produce constant excitement in a church is based on a perceived connection between amusement and success. Distractions—gimmicks—serve a church's marketing strategy. After all, if churches hold forth an undiluted commitment to the gospel of Christ Jesus, would anyone really be interested in that?

Can you spot the problems with the amusement approach to church growth? Altering the gospel will result in people believing something that isn't the gospel, and a non-gospel message doesn't save sinners. Furthermore, a non-gospel message doesn't help believers grow in a healthy way. Since the gospel is for both unbelievers and believers, we must not alter it. People naturally reject the gospel message, but Paul knew that every other message was powerless. Paul was unashamed of the gospel because it alone was the power of God for the salvation of sinners (Rom. 1:16). We're not helping the souls of those who gather if our focus is on something powerless.

Drawing people to church services with non-gospel strategies is dangerous because people will stay for what they came for. We must be careful never to put Christian discipleship on the back burner of the ministry strategy to increase the number of church attenders. If people come for the music style rather than for Jesus Christ, they may leave when the style changes. If people come because other attenders look and think like them, they may leave if the congregation becomes more diverse.

The gospel is not a product. It is not something we should seek to cleverly package, nor is it something leaders should alter for the sake of a more palatable message. The customer is not always right. The gospel is a nonnegotiable message, and it needs no alterations or amendments, no apologies or excuses. Rather than a product, the gospel is *power*—power to save sinners from eternal judgment in hell under the wrath of God.

When People Become Consumers

When church leaders apply a business mentality to ministry, they view people as consumers rather than worshipers who need to grow in the gospel and obey the commission to take that gospel to the nations. Keeping consumers satisfied becomes the top priority. They may leave your church for another if they're unhappy.

In our daily lives, we may appreciate and expect efficiency, punctuality, professionalism, and satisfaction from others. We certainly want these things in a business. And Sunday morning consumers may bring these expectations to church. Rather than countering the consumer mentality of churchgoers, many churches reinforce it. Sometimes we might not even exit the building before evaluating the service with me-centered questions: *Did I like the sermon? Did I enjoy the music? Did anyone speak to me today and ask how I was doing? Did I sit in my regular spot, or did some visitor take it?*

People who attend with a consumer mentality evaluate church with consumeristic questions, but people who come to worship the Lord and fellowship with his people must ask themselves different questions. *Did I make a joyful noise from my heart? Did I think about the words I was singing? Did I try to learn that new song? Did I focus on the sermon and follow along in my Bible? What did I learn from the passage that I should apply to my life this week? Did I seek out the new visitor and introduce myself? Did I approach a leader to volunteer for the upcoming church project?*

Which approach fits your church? Which approach do *you* have? Since the gospel is not a product, churches should not treat people like consumers. If keeping people happy isn't the main task of church leaders, then the church is free to fulfill its real purpose—to glorify God by edifying a worshipful body of believers who will make disciples and herald the gospel throughout the world.

You won't glorify God if your main focus is keeping people happy. Church leaders have to be prepared to let people leave. While ministers and other church members should encourage them to remain for biblical reasons and serve the body as Spirit-led and Spirit-gifted believers, you still can't keep everybody. Churches that only want to keep people will inevitably compromise the health of the church.

Paul was outraged that the Corinthian church had maintained fellowship with an unrepentant professing Christian when they should have expelled him (1 Cor. 5:1–11). But consumers don't receive harsh treatment well from their suppliers. They don't appreciate judgment on their lives, and they certainly don't tolerate expulsion from their church marketplace. It's impossible to reinforce a business mentality and pursue biblical church health. Not everyone will be happy with churches that pursue such health, and over time some people will inevitably leave. People will probably misperceive your intentions, too, but churches should think more about fearing God than fearing people. It is his church, not ours.

When Appeal Becomes the Priority

A church that pushes a product will inevitably become a competitor in the marketplace of worship gatherings. That makes *appeal* a crucial strategy in growing churches. If you draw believers to church with something other than the gospel, you must ensure that your amenities are more appealing than what's offered at the church down the street. If not, you may lose your consumer to another seller. You must maintain a competitive edge over other churches. The gospel is not the focus, and image is king.

When churches compete instead of cooperate, the Lord is not pleased. The spirit of competition results in sheep-steeling—drawing a person or family from one church to another. While growth is desirable in churches, conversion growth is more preferable than transfer growth. The number of people in the entire body of Christ doesn't increase when members move from one local church to another.

Churches shouldn't be against transfer growth, but growth strategies that focus on luring believers from one church to another reinforce the practice of church-hopping. A *church-hopper* is someone who moves from one church to another because of the power of appeal. Churches with a marketing mindset try to be unique and innovative, offering what no one else does for the sake of attracting more members. Drawn by the flash and sparkle of non-gospel amenities, people may join in droves—at least for a time, until the church down the road offers something better.

Church leaders must be discerning with strategies for growth. Methods matter, but preserving the truth of the gospel through integrity matters more. A well-intended statement such as "We need to get people into the church any way we can" isn't biblical. A well-known statement, "Methods can change, but the message must stay the same," sounds good but isn't biblical either. The end doesn't justify the means, and methods affect the message. As Mark Dever and Paul Alexander explain, "The methods we use to plant and water in God's vineyard must be subservient to and in complete harmony with the working of God's growth method—the Gospel, as faithfully preached by His servants. Working contrary to God's processes often means working contrary to His purposes."[1] Paul said, "But we have renounced disgraceful, underhanded ways. We refuse to practice cunning or to tamper with God's word, but by the open statement of the truth we would commend ourselves to everyone's conscience in the sight of God" (2 Cor. 4:2).

---

1. Mark Dever and Paul Alexander, *The Deliberate Church: Building Your Ministry on the Gospel* (Wheaton, IL: Crossway Books, 2005), 28.

When Numbers Become the Measurement

In the business world, numbers equal success. The more products a buyer purchases, the more money the seller makes—more, more, more. Churches that operate with a marketing mentality evaluate success in terms of numbers. And numbers aren't insignificant, for people being saved and believers joining churches have an effect on numbers. But using numbers as the measuring stick for ministry success is another matter. Churches with high attendance, big buildings, and large budgets are deemed successful churches—but successful in whose eyes?

While many large churches pursue biblical worship, preaching, and discipleship, a large crowd in a large building does not guarantee God's blessing. While some small churches aren't reaching their community through evangelism, preaching the gospel from the pulpit, or trying to expand their resources for work in God's kingdom, there are small churches that *are* doing these things. A small church is no indication of a ministry not blessed by God.

Paul warned that a time would come when people would not tolerate sound doctrine but would gather teachers around them who would say what their itching ears wanted to hear (2 Tim. 4:3). Large crowds may not gather for the sake of the true gospel and the true Lord. They may congregate where sin isn't confronted, where hard teachings and doctrines aren't expounded, and where Christianity-lite is practiced. Telling people what they want to hear might spike attendance, but dishonoring God is a sure result.

If we assume that church growth is up to us, we will look for methods and formulas to make success happen. Can church growth be engineered? Maybe if leaders nail the right programs, the right staff, the right location, and the right music, true growth will occur. In fact, maybe if your church isn't growing numerically, you're doing something wrong. DeYoung and Kluck write, "The fix-the-church books almost always figure that declining attendance, even as a percentage of the total population, means the church has messed something up....They still operate with the same basic assumption: namely, that churches should be growing and something is wrong with the church that isn't. This assumption, however, is alien to the New Testament."[2]

It is conceivable for a church to be faithful to God and not experience booming numerical growth. Growth isn't always numerical, right? How do numbers measure deeper love for Christ? How do you measure holiness? How do you present the fruit of the Spirit on charts and graphs? If God intends churches to be healthy and grow into maturity, we should ask ourselves whether God's priority is our priority. Many churches focus on what impresses the world. God is not impressed.

The Strategy of the Gospel

We need to discern between true and false understandings of how church growth happens. Careful reflection is especially necessary in a culture of instant gratification. There are no shortcuts to church growth and no hidden formulas. There is, however, a strategy that ministers should employ—and it's neither a mystery nor new.

Healthy church growth is inseparably connected to the gospel—an ancient message already revealed. At first, preaching the gospel may result in fewer attendees instead of more. But what if true growth happens after an initial consolidation and shrinking of the church? The gospel achieves God's purposes, and healthy church growth is rooted in it.

Paul told the Ephesian elders, "And now I commend you to God and to the word of his grace, which is able to build you up and to give you the inheritance among all those who are sanctified" (Acts 20:32). The "word of his grace" is the gospel message, the news of God's grace shown to sinners in sending Jesus as their sufficient substitute. This word of grace, Paul says, can build you up. He knew the Ephesian Christians would grow if they remained committed to the gospel. If they departed from the gospel, they would not grow. Forsaking the gospel reveals a false faith (1 Cor. 15:2; Gal. 1:6–7).

False gospels destroy, but the true gospel builds up. Paul told the Corinthians to be careful how they build (1 Cor. 3:10) because foundations

---

2. DeYoung and Kluck, *Why We Love the Church*, 31.

and materials matter. The church's foundation is Jesus Christ (1 Cor. 3:11). And if Jesus is the foundation of the church, then healthy church growth occurs through means and methods that honor Jesus.

Paul wrote, "Now if anyone builds on the foundation with gold, silver, precious stones, wood, hay, straw—each one's work will become manifest, for the Day will disclose it, because it will be revealed by fire, and the fire will test what sort of work each one has done" (1 Cor. 3:12–13). Paul uses two triplets, "gold, silver, precious stones" and "wood, hay, straw," to indicate durability (or lack thereof) and quality (or lack thereof). The return of Christ—"the Day"—will reveal the quality of our ministry labors and methods. Therefore, churches should be cautious with strategies aimed at fostering growth, for the return of Christ is sure. On that day, it will become clear whether these strategies and efforts honored the foundation of Christ Jesus.

Don't waste your ministry. Church leaders should want the day of Christ's return to reveal the good qualities of their ministries and confirm their commitment to the gospel for the people of God. So with the church's foundation being Christ Jesus himself, build with gold, silver, and costly stones—build with the gospel. The gospel is the only strategy that corresponds to the nature of the foundation. If we marginalize the gospel in an attempt to build on the church's foundation, we will inevitably build with wood, hay, and straw, and our work will be consumed in the fire of Christ's return.

When the early church gathered, they weren't devoted to a non-gospel message. They devoted themselves to the apostles' teachings, and the Lord added to their numbers (Acts 2:42, 47). Though opposed, the believers never stopped proclaiming the good news that Jesus is the Christ (Acts 5:42). When believers scattered because of persecution in Jerusalem, some of them went to Gentiles in Antioch, telling them about the Lord Jesus, and many people believed the message and turned to Christ (Acts 11:20–21). Through the Word, God built—and builds—the church. We need to preach the gospel and trust the Lord with the results.

The Giver of Growth

Results. Everyone wants results, and a marketing mindset says that your church is unsuccessful without them. But who really brings about these results? Paul says to the Corinthians, "I planted, Apollos watered, but God gave the growth" (1 Cor. 3:6). The truth is not hidden beneath layers of textual complexity. God grows his church. We plant and water and even build (1 Cor. 3:10, 12–13; 2 Cor. 10:8; 13:10), but the work of growth belongs to God alone.

Think back to Acts 20:32. The reason Paul committed the Ephesian elders to God and the gospel is because God works through the gospel to build up his people. You can't commit to God while forsaking the gospel. And commitment to the gospel is not without dependence on the God whose Son is the content of the good news—God *and* the gospel.

We're called to faithfulness in the service of Christ's church. Through the faithful teaching of the Word, God will save sinners and mature his people. We will encourage the downcast and give hope to the despairing. Paul told Timothy to endure hardship and discharge the duties of his ministry (2 Tim. 4:5). Stay the course and be faithful. Paul himself was an example of this faithfulness. Near the end of his life he said, "I have fought the good fight, I have finished the race, I have kept the faith" (2 Tim. 4:7).

Sometimes results don't happen quickly, if at all. No pastor is eager to sign up for the commission God gave Isaiah: "Go, and say to this people: 'Keep on hearing, but do not understand; keep on seeing, but do not perceive.' Make the heart of this people dull, and their ears heavy, and blind their eyes; lest they see with their eyes, and hear with their ears, and understand with their hearts, and turn and be healed" (Isa. 6:9–10). Isaiah had to preach to people he *knew* wouldn't listen. God chose to judge the people of Israel instead of opening their eyes and ears to the message, yet he still sent Isaiah to them. That would be a tough pastorate indeed!

Other times, growth happens slowly. Healthy church growth is often gradual, sometimes even inconsistent, requiring endurance and faithfulness from church leaders. Patience is not dispensable. Watching a seed grow into something magnificent doesn't happen overnight. But in our world of smartphones and laptops, patience and gradual progress aren't valued highly. Perhaps we should respond to our culture of instant gratification by planting a seed in some soil and learning a lesson about the kingdom of God.

Since God grants the growth, it's not helpful to expect something of ourselves that God doesn't expect. He doesn't tell us to grow his church, but he does call us to be faithful. He does tell us to preach the gospel. He does tell us to plant, water, and build with materials that correspond to the quality of the church's foundation, Jesus Christ. But the results are in his very capable hands.

Still Planting and Watering

Though God grants growth, planting and watering are not unimportant. God uses means to accomplish his ends. Paul reminded the Corinthians that he planted the seed and Apollos watered it (1 Cor. 3:6). But since God grows his people, we must understand the limits of our planting and watering. This means we must factor in human depravity as we conceive of church ministry. Only God can save a sinner's soul. Only God can open the eyes of the spiritually blind. Only God can shine light into the dark heart of the unbeliever. If leaders do not understand that no human gimmicks or methods can coerce, influence, or manipulate the unbeliever's dead heart to respond to Christ, they may try all manner of things to get saving results.

The problem with sinners isn't that they haven't heard the right speaker, that they haven't heard a certain type of music, or that the annual revival hasn't been scheduled. The problem with sinners is spiritual deadness, and the power of salvation is in the gospel of Christ Jesus. Let us proclaim the gospel and minister with the gospel. Do you have a low view of the gospel's power? Do you think it's insufficient or irrelevant to church growth? Do you believe there's a more powerful or more capable method?

Church leaders might show, inadvertently, that in their growth methods they are quite ashamed of the gospel. Could the problem be in part that a church thinks its primary role is to *draw* rather than *go*? In event-based evangelism, churches must be constantly drawing the lost to their meetings and gatherings. Primarily, however, churches must be a going people—going into neighborhoods, communities, cities, states, countries, and continents. Jesus commissioned and empowered his people to go to the lost (Matt. 28:19–20; Acts 1:8).

Ministering in an American culture averse to religious institutions, churches must face the truth that most unbelievers will not come to their events, no matter what they say or do to draw them. And moving unbelievers from outside the church to inside the church is pointless if the true gospel isn't proclaimed to them. Shouldn't they be building relationships with unbelievers with the prayer and hope for gospel opportunities? Planting and watering aren't instantaneous activities. Loving and caring for the souls of others takes time and sacrifice. We need the gospel to shape the way we serve and care for the believers in our churches. And we need the gospel to shape the way we relate to those who don't yet know Christ.

Who are you investing in? When is the last time you had an unbeliever in your home? Who are the unbelievers you're praying for? Can you identify ways you're planting and watering in the lives of others?

The Goal in Gathered Worship

Since the gospel should drive our ministries and methods, and since our planting and watering are dependent on God who gives the growth, we are free to make much of God in corporate worship on the Lord's Day. We don't need gimmicks. We don't need to foster atmospheres of amusement. The reason the saints gather is *God*.

Our church services should prioritize the praise of God (Ps. 95:1–11; Col. 3:16). Our churches should prioritize the reading, preaching, and teaching of scripture (1 Tim. 4:13). The aim is to build up the church with the practice of faithfully preaching the scriptures to God's people. Through preaching, we're calling listeners to reckon with God's revelation of himself. We want to gather under God's Word with hearts of glad submission and trust. Sound doctrine is not peripheral or expendable.

We may draw people into church if we design self-centered services, but we will not honor the Lord. Sinners are not helped by the reinforcement of their self-centeredness. God-centered singing and preaching confront the unbeliever with the truth of who God is and what he has done. We should gather intentionally to make much of God. Since only believers offer pleasing worship to God and receive edification from his Word, corporate worship is mainly for believers. Unbelievers will probably be present, but they are not the focus. This truth should be obvious to us since unbelievers aren't part of the body of Christ nor do they know the God we worship.

Even though the gathering of the saints is for the saints, we should still seek to build relationships with unbelieving attenders, making the most of opportunities to explain the gospel to them. Hopefully, in the corporate reading and preaching of scripture, unbelievers will hear about who God is and what he has done. It is wise for preachers to incorporate basic gospel truths into each sermon for the sake of any unbelievers who are present and know little about the Christian faith. Factoring in the presence of unbelievers is not the same as focusing on the unbeliever in the design of the corporate service. Some churches tend to make the presence of unbelievers a determinative factor in what takes place during the service. This sensitivity might include avoiding difficult biblical topics—the wrath of God, repentance from sin, suffering in the Christian life—so unbelievers aren't uncomfortable.

But attempts to make unbelievers comfortable may not be helpful to their souls. Consider the nature of worship. The saints sing to their holy God who is worthy of all praise and has delivered them from the penalty and power of sin. If unbelievers come into the presence of God who is being worshiped by his people, shouldn't this make them, to some degree, *uncomfortable*? Shouldn't we hope that unbelievers leave a church service feeling convicted instead of amused? Shouldn't we want them pondering the weight and glory of the gathering of people they were just among?

Knowing that unbelievers need to hear the gospel more than anything else makes it devastating to think that churches seek to accommodate unbelievers in everything from sermon topics and musical styles to attire and amenities. While well-intended, these efforts are misguided. Our understanding of human depravity is crucial to this subject. If we believe that the problem with unbelievers is that their hearts are spiritually dead, then no manner of church appeal can influence them toward God. Unbelievers who come to church aren't seeking God because no one seeks God apart from the power of Christ and the work of his Spirit (John 6:44; Rom. 3:11–12).

Though church is mainly for believers, it is not wrong for unbelievers to see the saints worship God and hear from his Word. We should not exclude unbelievers from attending services. We must remember, however, that the exaltation of God is the goal of our assembly. Corporate worship is what *believers* do.

Not Spectators but Worshipers

Believers shouldn't attend church with a spectator mindset. Corporate worship requires the active engagement of the saints in four primary areas: praying, singing, giving, and listening. First, believers should pray corporately. Corporate prayer means that the listeners are mentally engaged in prayers voiced to God. I didn't always understand the purpose of corporate prayer. When I was a kid in church, I hardly paid attention to the content of someone praying in public. They weren't talking to me, right? But corporate prayer isn't an occasion for people to focus less on what is said. Corporate prayer is for the participation of saints who can season the intercession with affirmations of thanksgiving, blessing, and praise.

Second, believers should join together in singing to God. Singing isn't something you watch your music director, praise band, or choir do. Paul says to address one another "in psalms and hymns and spiritual songs, singing and making melody to the Lord with your heart" (Eph. 5:19). In singing, we exalt God and educate one another. Corporate singing is theological education. Singing involves instructing, exhorting, and reminding other believers about God's character and mighty deeds, especially through songs about the cross. Some believers may feel nervous to sing in front of others, they may feel awkward if they don't know a certain song, or they may feel insecure about the sound of their voice. Despite any insecurities, believers should count it a privilege to sing with the saints in a gathered assembly. Before congregational singing, it may be helpful to pray for your soul. Ask God to fill your heart with gratitude and joy. Ask him to help your love for him overcome any feelings of awkwardness or embarrassment. Ask him to help you see that joining in corporate worship is an act of obedience. Ask him to help you cast your eyes from yourself to his worth.

Third, believers should participate in worship through giving. The New Testament sets a precedent for giving to ministers and missionaries (1 Cor. 16:1–4; 2 Cor. 8:1–9; Rom. 15:24), supporting your church's pastors and teachers (1 Cor. 9:9–12; 1 Tim. 5:17–18), giving to those in need (Matt. 6:1–4), and demonstrating through material sacrifice where your treasure truly is (Matt. 6:19–21). In our materialistic culture, this call to financially invest in your church and its various ministers and ministries may seem demanding. But consider what Jesus said. "No one can serve two masters, for either he will hate the one and love the other, or he will be devoted to the one and despise the other. You cannot serve God and money" (Matt. 6:24). Giving is not something only radical Christians do. Financial generosity was characteristic of the early church (Acts 2:44–45; 4:34–35). Such generosity must have puzzled outsiders who loved money and possessions. We should pray for hearts of cheerful generosity, for God loves a cheerful giver (2 Cor. 9:7).

Fourth, believers should actively listen to the sermon. Unfortunately, some people listen to sermons the same way they watch television—passive and disengaged with little, if any, reflection. Listening that honors the Lord involves active engagement of the mind and prayerful dependence on the Spirit—all with the intention to obey the message (James 1:22). Sermons aren't preached for mindless consumption. But let's face the truth that we won't remember most of what we hear. Why, then, should you actively listen? The point of active engagement isn't to retain everything you hear. The point is being prayerfully dependent on the Spirit to engage God's truth and then apply it to your life. You may not remember most of what shapes you, but that doesn't change the fact that it has still shaped you. A man once said to his friend, "I don't want to listen to any more sermons. I don't remember them anyway." His friend responded, "Well, do you remember what your wife cooked for dinner a week ago?" The man thought for a moment and said no. His friend said, "You might not remember what she cooked, but you're still alive because you ate it." Active listening to the Word that is preached feeds our souls and sustains our faith.

Conclusion

The church is not a business, and the gospel is not a product to be pushed and marketed. The gospel is the power of God for salvation, and it is vital to church ministry and church growth. We're called to be faithful while trusting God with the results of all our planting and watering work. Our labors are not in vain because God is sovereign, wise, and good. With the power of the gospel at work in our ministries, we are free to be unashamed of the good news and hold unwaveringly to its truth. We shouldn't think of church attenders as consumers. Our attenders are sinners in need of saving grace, and we have the message about that grace. When we gather on the Lord's Day, we do so for the glory of God's name. As we pray, sing, give, and listen together, the Spirit is at work through his Word. What have we to fear?

8
THE WHOLE WORLD IN HIS PLANS

Jesus commissioned his disciples to make disciples (Matt. 28:19–20). This is the church's mission, and all other endeavors are secondary. An intentional approach to disciple-making may require rethinking your ministry. The gospel is a global message worthy of a global mindset. We need a gospel-shaped perspective that desires and endeavors (through going and giving) to send the good news to every nation and people group in the world. God's heart is for the nations. Unless believers develop a mindset that wants the good news to make a global impact, they will not be thinking with a missionary mindset that reflects God's heart.

The Blessing for the Nations

God's global mission dominates the Bible from beginning to end. In the first book of the Bible, God promises a blessing for all people. He told Abraham, "And I will make of you a great nation, and I will bless you and make your name great, so that you will be a blessing. I will bless those who bless you, and him who dishonors you I will curse, and in you all the families of the earth shall be blessed" (Gen. 12:2–3). Paul echoed God's promise when he wrote, "Know then that it is those of faith who are the sons of Abraham. And the Scripture, foreseeing that God would justify the Gentiles by faith, preached the gospel beforehand to Abraham, saying, 'In you shall all the nations be blessed'" (Gal. 3:7–8).

The global gospel is glimpsed and rooted in Genesis. God fulfilled his promise to bless all nations by sending Jesus for all people. The fullest experience of the blessing promised to Abraham is salvation through Christ alone (Gal. 3:9–14). If you belong to Christ, you are a child of Abraham, and if you are a child of Abraham, you are an heir of God's promises.

Praise from the Nations

Through the power of the gospel, God is raising up true worshipers from the nations. In the book of Psalms, we find abundant evidence that the nations should worship God. Even the shortest psalm has a global agenda: "Praise the LORD, all nations! Extol him, all peoples! For great is his steadfast love toward us, and the faithfulness of the LORD endures forever. Praise the LORD!" (Ps. 117:1–2). The psalmist doesn't list any exceptions to this sweeping command.

The last verse in the book of Psalms says, "Let everything that has breath praise the LORD! Praise the LORD!" (Ps. 150:6). Every person breathing in the world has a responsibility to worship the Maker of heaven and earth, for God is great and worthy to be praised (Ps. 48:1). The psalmist calls us to proclaim God's salvation in a new song, to proclaim his glory and deeds among all people (Ps. 96:1–3). The anthem of the nations should be "The LORD reigns!" (Ps. 96:10).

God has displayed his greatness and the glory of his name for all to see. He has set his glory above the heavens (Ps. 8:1), and he has declared his glory in the heavens (Ps. 19:1). Everyone in the world has the so-called book of natural revelation open to them night and day, which is why everyone is without excuse in their idolatry (Rom. 1:20). Seeing the stars should fill us with worship toward God. Beholding the mountains should stir us with praise to God. Watching a sunrise should prompt awe and wonder at God. But human wickedness suppresses the truth of God's greatness (Rom. 1:18). God's revelation has not been subtle, but neither has people's rejection of it (Rom. 1:19–20).

Light for the Gentiles

Though the nations were darkened in their understanding about the truth and worth of the living God, the dawning of God's salvation came in

Christ. The prophet Isaiah predicted that the Servant of the Lord would be a light for the Gentiles so salvation would spread to the ends of the earth (Isa. 49:6). This delivering figure would extend God's glory to the nations. Jesus—the Servant whom Isaiah promised—said, "I am the light of the world" (John 8:12). The coming of Christ was the dawning of salvation.

Centuries after the prophet Isaiah, a man named Simeon held baby Jesus and said, "Lord, now you are letting your servant depart in peace, according to your word; for my eyes have seen your salvation that you have prepared in the presence of all peoples, a light for revelation to the Gentiles, and for glory to your people Israel" (Luke 2:29–32). Simeon said he was witnessing the fulfillment of the hopes in Isaiah's prophecy (see Isa. 9:1–2). The narrator of John's Gospel concurred: "In him was life, and the life was the light of men. The light shines in the darkness, and the darkness has not overcome it" (John 1:4–5). Jesus was born to be the light and Savior of the nations.

Commission to the Nations

The promised Savior gave a commission that corresponded to the scope of God's redemptive plan. God's plan for the nations meant a commission to the nations. In Matthew 28:19, Jesus commissioned the church to make disciples of all nations, baptizing them and teaching them the faith. Though Matthew's Gospel contains the well-known Great Commission, Luke's Gospel ends with the same theme, "that repentance for the forgiveness of sins should be proclaimed in his name to all nations, beginning from Jerusalem" (Luke 24:47). In Luke's second volume, the book of Acts, he recorded Jesus's words about Spirit empowerment: "But you will receive power when the Holy Spirit has come upon you, and you will be my witnesses in Jerusalem and in all Judea and Samaria, and to the end of the earth" (Acts 1:8). In the power of the Spirit, the disciples would bear witness to Jesus by proclaiming the gospel throughout the world.

With a heart for Jews and Gentiles, Paul understood his mission in light of Jesus's role as the Servant from Isaiah's prophecy. Paul told the Jews in Pisidian Antioch, "For so the Lord has commanded us, saying, 'I have made you a light for the Gentiles, that you may bring salvation to the ends of the earth'" (Acts 13:47, see Isa. 49:6). Jesus's mission continued through Paul's mission. Jesus sent Paul to the nations "to open their eyes, so that they may turn from darkness to light and from the power of Satan to God, that they may receive forgiveness of sins and a place among those who are sanctified by faith in me" (Acts 26:17–18).

Paul thought of his missionary labors as embodying the sufferings and death of Christ (2 Cor. 4:10; Col. 1:24). The commission to the church is not a different mission from what the suffering Servant—Jesus—embodied and advanced. Disciples take up the mission of their Lord, becoming suffering servants of the suffering Servant. Since Jesus carried the light of his message to Jews and Gentiles, his followers did—and do—the same.

In the final book of scripture, the apostle John gives the reader glimpses of worldwide worship. Living creatures and elders sing to Jesus, "Worthy are you to take the scroll and to open its seals, for you were slain, and by your blood you ransomed people for God from every tribe and language and people and nation, and you have made them a kingdom and priests to our God, and they shall reign on the earth" (Rev. 5:9–10). John also portrays a great multitude from all tribes and peoples clothed in white robes and singing praise, ascribing their salvation to God (Rev. 7:9–10). The gospel is global because the design of redemption was global.

No Other Name

There is one gospel, and God entrusted his church with the commission to take this message to everyone everywhere. Examining the speeches and letters of the apostles yields a consistent teaching that only Jesus is the Savior of sinners, so we must repent from sin and trust in him.

As the events of Acts unfolded, the apostles experienced increasing opposition from the Jewish leadership. When Peter and John were teaching people in Jerusalem about the risen Jesus, members of the Sadducees arrested them and put them in jail (Acts 4:1–3). The next day, Peter and John appeared before the Sanhedrin to answer questions (Acts 4:7). In his speech, Peter proclaimed the exclusivity of the gospel message by denying that salvation is outside the name of Jesus: "And there is salvation in no one else, for there is no other name under heaven given among men by which we must be saved" (Acts 4:12).

No other name. This provokes an important question: Can people be saved if they don't believe in Christ? People don't arrive at saving revelation apart from hearing the true gospel, and only the gospel of Jesus announces God's saving work on behalf of sinners. Paul said that everyone who calls on the name of Christ will be saved (Rom. 10:13). But Paul understood the urgency of the Christian mission. If sinners cannot be saved unless they call on Jesus, "how then will they call on him in whom they have not believed? And how are they to believe in him of whom they have never heard? And how are they to hear without someone preaching?" (Rom. 10:14).

Piper sees the implication of Paul's reasoning: "This rules out the argument that a person might have saving faith without really knowing or meeting Christ in the gospel....This rules out the argument that one might somehow meet Christ or hear Christ without a messenger to tell the gospel."[1] The church must proclaim Jesus to the nations, or the nations cannot be saved. There is no other name, and there is no other way. Jesus claimed, "I am the way, and the truth, and the life. No one comes to the Father except through me" (John 14:6).

Those Who Have Never Heard

It is commonly believed that people who have never heard of Jesus aren't necessarily condemned. Perhaps God can reveal himself to them through their religion. Could it be that people who have never had a chance to hear about Jesus will be saved some other way? Maybe people who are sincerely seeking truth will be saved because of the light of revelation they have embraced. These notions may stem from a reluctance to believe that people who never hear the gospel will be condemned by God. Does it seem

---

1. John Piper, *Let the Nations Be Glad! The Supremacy of God in Missions,* Rev. Ed. (Grand Rapids, MI: Baker Academic, 2003), 145.

unjust to you that God will condemn people who have never heard of Jesus? I want to tell you why it's not.

God condemns sinners on the basis of their sin, not on the basis of whether they have heard the gospel. Judgment is according to works: "And the sea gave up the dead who were in it, Death and Hades gave up the dead who were in them, and they were judged, each of them, according to what they had done" (Rev. 20:13). It is not unjust for God to condemn sinners even though they have never heard the gospel.

Unlike judgment, salvation is based on God's grace. While people can be condemned without ever hearing the gospel, no one can be saved without it. Judgment is based on works; salvation is based on grace. The fact that many unbelievers may never hear the gospel does not leave God without a basis to condemn them at the judgment. Sinners come into this world condemned already and are objects of God's wrath (John 3:18, 36; Eph. 2:3). We need to expose the false assumption that God's basis of condemnation is whether people have rejected the gospel. God does not lack a basis for the righteous condemnation of sinners.

Let's look at this issue from another perspective. If people who never heard the gospel could still be saved while people who reject the gospel will be condemned, wouldn't it be better for everyone if Christians *stopped* sharing the gospel with unbelievers? That way, no one could reject the gospel and be condemned.

Some people believe that natural revelation in creation can lead people to the knowledge of saving truth. People throughout the world worship something. Though religious practices may not be Christian, maybe people are doing the best they can with the light they have. Maybe sinners are responsible for how they respond to the light of truth they have been shown. All this is an interesting theory, but is it biblical? Can sinners be saved by any light of truth other than the light of knowing Jesus Christ?

Romans 1 is helpful here. God's eternal power and divine nature can be affirmed by beholding creation, so people are without excuse in these matters (Rom. 1:19–20). Creation demonstrates the presence of a Creator—specifically that this Creator is divine and powerful. But in response to this knowledge, sinful people did not glorify God but became futile in their thinking and darkened in their foolish hearts (Rom. 1:21). Natural revelation in creation does not lead sinful people to worship God. Instead, people reject the truth and embrace the foolishness of idolatry.

When Paul says sinners "are without excuse" (Rom. 1:20), he affirms that God justly judges sinners for rejecting the truth displayed in God's creation. People should glorify God, but they don't. Sinners preferred to exchange the glory of God for images and idols (Rom. 1:23). When you see people worshiping idols, that devotion is not proof they are seeking God. Idolatry is proof they are rebelling against God. They wanted a lie instead of the truth (Rom. 1:25). Serving created things means *not* serving the Creator. Ignorant worship is not true worship. Natural revelation, then, doesn't have redemptive power. Since embracing falsehood doesn't honor God, no one should conclude that any idolatry can give enough light for people to be saved. The path of falsehood doesn't lead to truth, only to further deception and delusion. The people who worship other gods aren't manifesting their love for truth but rather their tragic embrace of falsehood.

While it may be comforting to believe that sincere followers of other religions can be saved through the revelatory light of creation without ever hearing the true gospel of Jesus Christ, this notion contradicts scripture. Creation does communicate truth about God, but natural revelation is sufficient only to condemn—not save—sinners.

Repent and Believe—or Perish

Athens was a city full of idols, and Paul was angry when he saw it with his own eyes (Acts 17:16). He told some of the Athenians that they were religious but didn't know the true God (Acts 17:22–23). They had expressed their idolatrous hearts by worshiping objects fashioned by human hands (Acts 17:29). Despite the widespread worship of idols, Paul denied that such devotion pleased God. He said God "commands all people everywhere to repent" (Acts 17:30). *All people. Everywhere.*

Paul's words in Acts 17 confirm his words at the beginning of Romans. Ignorant worship is idolatry, not true worship. All sinners received the same message from Paul: repent of sin and trust in Jesus Christ, or perish. Paul warned the Athenians that God "has fixed a day on which he will judge the world in righteousness by a man whom he has appointed; and of this he has given assurance to all by raising him from the dead" (Acts 17:31). Everyone will know Jesus either as their savior or their judge.

While Paul's gospel message was the same for everyone, he didn't always begin the same way. In Acts 17, he began with the doctrines of God and creation since Athens was full of polytheism and pantheism. Athenian Gentiles needed to know the basic teachings about the one true God. This is an important starting place even in contemporary polytheistic cultures. For example, during mission trips to Thailand, our teams proclaimed Jesus as the only Lord and Savior so the Thai Buddhists would not mistakenly add Jesus to their growing list of names esteemed in ancestor worship. Unbelievers must understand that worship is due to Christ alone.

In Acts 13, when Paul spoke with Jews and God-fearers at Pisidian Antioch, he began with Jewish history and showed how Jesus fulfilled the promises that God made to Israel. He taught them that even their rejection of Jesus was in accord with God's Word (Acts 13:27). He then argued that Jesus's resurrection fulfilled God's promises (Acts 13:33–35; see Ps. 2:7; 16:10; Isa. 55:3).

Looking at Acts 13 and 17, we can see that Paul began his sermons with theological issues pertaining to his specific audience. Jews and pagans approached life from different perspectives. Jews were monotheistic, most of them believed in an end-time resurrection of the dead, and they agreed that God would fulfill the prophecies of scripture. On the other hand, pagans didn't anticipate a bodily resurrection, they weren't concerned whether God would keep his promises to the Israelites, and they were polytheistic and pantheistic in their worldview.

While Paul didn't always begin his messages in the same way, he still preached the gospel to his hearers. To the Jews at Pisidian Antioch, he announced that there is forgiveness of sins through Jesus (Acts 13:38–39). To the Athenian Jews, he spoke about repentance and the resurrection of Jesus (Acts 17:30–31). Paul's commitment to evangelism didn't involve altering the gospel for the sake of winning Jews and Gentiles. Different audiences, same gospel. Different locations, same gospel. Different opening theological issues, same gospel.

Thinking of God's Worth

Perhaps there is no more urgent awareness than the world's need for the gospel, a message billions of people have not embraced. Thinking locally is good, but it is insufficient. Christians must think globally about the gospel. Since Christians know the joy of worshiping the true and living God, they should want everyone to worship him. He is worthy of worldwide worship, and his glory and renown should fill the whole earth. Therefore, Christians should not be indifferent to the nations; they should long to see every tribe and tongue offer true worship to God. Global thinking is for the glory of God.

Piper reminds us, "Missions is not the ultimate goal of the church. Worship is. Missions exists because worship doesn't."[2] Though worldwide worship of the triune God isn't happening, it should be. The Father gave the Son the name that is above every name so that at the name of Jesus every knee should bow (Phil. 2:9–11). In the future, everyone will acknowledge the lordship and authority of Jesus, but some people will never worship Jesus. They will be rebels forever. Bowing the knee to Jesus is an acknowledgment of his authority, but worship comes from the heart. Those who remain unbelievers will never have hearts that warm in worship to God.

Though Paul speaks of a day when every tongue will confess the lordship of Jesus, not every heart will be filled with wonder and reverence for the person of Jesus Christ. The powers of darkness will bow their defeated knees, and the reign and power of Jesus will be evident to everyone. But at that time it will be too late for any unbeliever to be saved.

---

2. Piper, *Let the Nations Be Glad!* 17.

The Sovereignty of Jesus

In Matthew 28, Jesus's commission to make disciples of all nations includes the word *therefore* (Matt. 28:19). A well-known adage applies—if you see a *therefore*, ask what it is *there for*. Jesus introduces the command after laying its foundation in the previous verse. The basis of the Great Commission is Jesus's extraordinary claim that "all authority in heaven and on earth has been given to me" (Matt. 28:18). Jesus is claiming sovereignty over everything.

While you could probably offer different reasons for global missions, has Jesus's comprehensive sovereignty ever stirred your obedience to make disciples? The scope of missions extends to the scope of Christ's sovereignty; he is sovereign over everyone, so everyone should submit to his lordship. If Jesus was not sovereign over all things, in whose authority could we take the gospel to the nations? If Jesus did not have all authority in heaven and on earth, what hope could there be for the gospel's advancement in the world? J. I. Packer is right: "Were it not for the sovereign grace of God, evangelism would be the most futile and useless enterprise that the world has ever seen, and there would be no more complete waste of time under the sun than to preach the Christian gospel."[3]

The Great Commission sends disciples into the world over which Jesus rules. He is Lord of every nation and every people group. Nothing in heaven and earth exists outside his total control. "So far from making evangelism pointless," Packer says, "the sovereignty of God in grace is the one thing that prevents evangelism from being pointless. For it creates the possibility—indeed, the certainty—that evangelism will be fruitful."[4] This reality should fill believers with courage. It takes boldness to go to the nations, and the sovereignty of Jesus is no small motivator.

Believers don't give their lives for the work of the gospel because they believe Jesus's lordship is in question. Christians don't risk the deaths of family and friends in other parts of the world because they doubt the power

---

3. J. I. Packer, *Evangelism and the Sovereignty of God* (Downers Grove, IL: IVP Books, 1961), 116.

4. Ibid.

of Jesus to spread his name and fame. People die for the gospel because they believe Jesus's promise that he will build his church (Matt. 16:18). Christians around the globe are willing to suffer loss of job, reputation, health, and safety because they agree with Paul that all things are rubbish compared to knowing Christ (Phil. 3:7).

The sovereignty of Jesus is our security in suffering and death. Jesus said to his disciples, "And do not fear those who kill the body but cannot kill the soul. Rather fear him who can destroy both soul and body in hell" (Matt. 10:28). What's the worst thing that can happen to a believer who proclaims the gospel? They could be killed—but nothing worse. Jesus has borne our condemnation through his substitutionary death on the cross.

If Jesus doesn't return first, we will all die. Those who try to preserve their own lives will find that in the end, they will lose what they seek to keep (Matt. 10:39). More important than your own life is the gospel. Should the time come, be like the believers of Revelation 12 who faced the raging of the dragon and the demand to compromise their faith. These believers refused to turn from Christ. Their allegiance was to him. They conquered the accuser "by the blood of the Lamb and by the word of their testimony, for they loved not their lives even unto death" (Rev. 12:11).

Many believers will face terrible emotional and physical turmoil. "You will be delivered up even by parents and brothers and relatives and friends, and some of you they will put to death. You will be hated by all for my name's sake" (Luke 21:16–17). The sovereignty of Jesus doesn't prevent us from suffering but preserves us through suffering. "But not a hair of your head will perish. By your endurance you will gain your lives" (Luke 21:18–19). The word *perish* refers to spiritual destruction since physical death is a possibility. Believers are spiritually secure in Christ, even if they suffer the loss of their family, friends, or head. *Not a hair of your head will perish.* Who could make such a promise except the One with all authority in heaven and earth?

A Matter of Obedience

In Matthew 28:19–20, Jesus didn't give his disciples the Great Option—he gave them the Great Commission. Making disciples of the nations is about obedience. His disciples should teach others to obey everything he commanded them (Matt. 28:20). But how can we teach the nations about obeying Jesus if we disobey him by not taking the gospel to them? Churches must be globally minded because obedience to Jesus is at stake. David Platt asks a key question: "Where in the Bible is missions ever identified as an optional program in the church?"[5]

There are local physical and spiritual needs in close proximity to you. Some church members have more financial struggles than others. Caring for the needs of widows isn't a concern that expired in Paul's day (1 Tim. 5:3, 9–10). James said that religion acceptable to God is to look after orphans and widows in their distress and to remain unpolluted by the world (James 1:27). Like me, you probably have friends and family who are unbelievers, and there may not be many, if any, Christians where you work. With so many needs near us, some believers think that local needs warrant the church's focus and resources.

But a global mindset doesn't exclude a concern for local needs. Instead, a closed local mindset excludes a concern for international needs. Platt is again helpful: "Certainly there are great needs here. But must we insist on dividing the Great Commission into an either-or proposition? Who told us that we had to choose to have a heart for the United States *or* a heart for the world?"[6] Churches should start their witness for Christ in their local communities, but they shouldn't stop there. Jesus told his disciples that "you will be my witnesses in Jerusalem and in all Judea and Samaria, and to the end of the earth" (Acts 1:8). Churches in America should have hearts for all nations.

How are you invested in taking the gospel to all nations? Some churches face practical obstacles and lack direct connections to missionaries, large budgets that allocate money to missions, leaders who promote a missions mindset

---

5. Platt, *Radical*, 72.
6. Ibid.

among church members, obvious opportunities to engage in global missions outside the country, and volunteers to travel to unfamiliar territories.

I want to suggest six practical steps to implement in your church toward the cultivation of a global missions mindset. First, pray for world missions. A church that doesn't pray for the spread of the gospel to all nations doesn't have a global mindset. The content of a church's prayers is an indication of its concerns. If the nations are on God's heart, then they should be on our hearts. And the burdens of our hearts show up in our prayers. The body of Christ should intercede for missionaries around the world who labor for the sake of the gospel. There are thousands of people groups who have never been infiltrated with the good news; they are totally unreached with no known believers or missionaries among them. Perhaps your church could emphasize an annual missions week during which the church could pray corporately and individually for the spread of the gospel around the world.

Second, talk about missionaries. Pastors can do this in sermons, incorporating stories of international missionaries. Learn about current opposition, persecution, martyrdom, and revival. Other leaders in your church who teach classes can frequently incorporate world missions into their lessons. Read stories about missionaries, learn their names, and spread this information to the people in your church. What your church spends time talking about also indicates its priority. Therefore, talking about missionaries can demonstrate a concern for the gospel's work in the world.

Third, encourage people to give to world missions. Some churches announce special times of giving during Christmas and Easter, and your church may see the value in adopting these emphases. Your church might also consider budgeting to support mission agencies and organizations. Such groups can often directly and discerningly distribute funds to international gospel work. Therefore, to support them is to support world missions. For example, many Southern Baptist churches support the North American Mission Board and the International Mission Board. Prayerfully discern how to allocate funds for the global spread of the gospel, and be open to new ways to raise funds for missions.

Fourth, develop direct connections with international missionaries. If no one in your church has a direct connection with one, then contact a church that does. Knowing the names of a missionary family, seeing their pictures, and receiving frequent updates can greatly contribute to the cultivation of a church's global mindset. By maintaining contact with full-time missionaries, your church will know the specific needs to bring to the Lord in prayer, as well as the conversions and growth for which to praise and thank him. Since international missionaries may take opportunities to visit families in their home countries, there may be a future opportunity to welcome those missionaries to your church for a time of personal visit, testimony, and edification. There's no one like an international missionary to help a church develop an international mindset.

Fifth, participate in short-term mission trips outside the United States. These trips are most effective when they are planned with a missionary who is already located in the country of interest. Such cooperation is important for the ongoing work in the other location so short-term mission teams don't unintentionally undermine the efforts of the vocational missionaries. Missionaries will feel supported and edified when teams arrive with hearts of service and submission. When the team returns home, they can bring reports of the power of God displayed in other parts of the world. These reports will encourage the senders and reinforce a global mindset in that church.

Sixth, frequently encourage the people in your church to prayerfully consider giving their lives to international missions. When the Lord guides believers into full-time mission work, they are probably involved in a church already—so why shouldn't it be yours? Pray that your church would be a context from which the Lord calls people to be missionaries. When pastors preach from scripture texts connected to the global nature of the gospel, they should exhort their listeners to prayerfully reflect on how the Lord wants them to be involved in international mission work—perhaps even to surrender their lives to vocational mission work.

If a church isn't doing all it can with its people and resources to make disciples of the nations, what is the barrier? Is it a lack of motivation? Is it the absence of a global mindset? Is it an explicit denial of responsibility? Is it an indifference to obedience? Is it an unhealthy focus on unimportant issues? May the Lord remind us that the nations will not glorify God because we organized a successful program but because we obeyed the Great Commission and took the gospel to people who need it.

Conclusion

Christians must be globally minded because the only hope for the nations is the Christ whom the gospel exalts. A global mindset is important because it corresponds to the scope of God's sovereignty and work in the world. We should care about the glory of God being displayed throughout the earth, and we should long to see the realization of the vision in the book of Revelation of nations worshiping God together. When unreached people hear and embrace the gospel of Jesus, it is a picture of Isaiah 9:2: "The people who walked in darkness have seen a great light"—the light of Jesus Christ that shines in the good news.

9
GOOD NEWS FOR THE HOME

We all live somewhere, and the good news needs to shine there as we walk in humble trust in and obedience to Jesus Christ. Whether Christians live alone, with parents, with a roommate, with a spouse, or with children, they should consider how the home is a crucial realm for their discipleship. Wherever and with whomever God has placed us in his providence, that is where we should flourish and be faithful.

A Place to Be Known

The home is a hard place to maintain pretense for very long. Our sins become obvious. Our struggles become known. Others are not blind to our blind spots. But this is good. Healthy self-knowledge is best cultivated in community with other people. And in relationship with others, we learn more about ourselves. The more we learn about ourselves, the more opportunities for growth will surface. Our relationships are part of God's sanctifying plan. The relationships in our lives require maintenance, patience, forgiveness, and investment.

How would those closest to you describe your commitment to Christ and your hope in the gospel? You should ask them. Do they consider you a devoted disciple? Would they say you love God's Word? Would they say you love God's people?

Home is where we put down roots, but that doesn't mean a static life. Our self is dynamic—responding to influences around us, changing and forming, growing and seeking. When we come to know Christ Jesus as our

Savior, we're changed, brought from darkness to light. And this transformation, this new status, will become evident to others around us. Would it surprise those closest to you that your allegiance is to Christ?

Designed for Community

We need one another if we're going to make it to the end. I don't mean Christ's grasp on us is loose or flimsy. But God's sanctifying plan for his people includes a matrix of relationships. God has designed us for community, and this design should shape our priorities and pursuits. We need to walk with other believers for the sake of our holiness and the labors of love.

Do you think you need other people? Do you see the church of Christ as indispensable for your life? Do you believe wise friends are vital for your spiritual health? Do you sense your own vulnerabilities and weaknesses to the degree that you need the strength and burden-sharing shoulders of gospel-loving friends?

Married people need fellowship with those who aren't married, and single people need fellowship with families. Don't make your current status and stage in life the model for the relationships you pursue. We need our homes to be strategic places of investment and involvement for Christ's kingdom. Your home can be a place God wields for his glory as you faithfully steward your time and resources on behalf of others.

Single and Single-Minded

Every status and stage in life has its own advantages and disadvantages. Writing about singleness, Paul says, "I want you to be free from anxieties. The unmarried man is anxious about the things of the Lord, how to please the Lord" (1 Cor. 7:32). The married man, on the other hand, is divided (1 Cor. 7:33–34). During temporary or lifelong singleness, the believer is able to focus on the things of Christ with a single-mindedness that would not be possible in other circumstances.

Single men and women are gifts of God to his church. They may have fewer constraints on their time, which can be deployed for building up the local church. They may be better positioned for spontaneous ministry opportunities. Singleness may allow international travel and missionary work that, in other circumstances, may not have been advisable or financially possible.

If you are single, your central identity is not your singleness. The most important thing about you is that you are in Christ through faith. The gift of salvation has secured your place with God's family. Being a son or daughter of God is *the* most important status we have. If we are in Christ, we are co-heirs of God's promises with a future of resurrection and glory. While contentment may be a temporary struggle in this world full of troubles, the presence of Christ with us is a comfort and assurance. We belong to his bride, and we are dearly loved.

Holiness in the Home

Whether we live alone or with others, God's will for our lives is our sanctification, "that you abstain from sexual immorality; that each one of you know how to control his own body in holiness and honor, not in the passion of lust like the Gentiles who do not know God" (1 Thess. 4:3–5). Is your home a place where righteousness is loved in the light or where sin is cherished in the dark?

Nothing you do in your home will ever escape the eyes of God. Are there sins of anger and selfishness in the home that need repentance? Are there sexual sins that need to be exposed and abandoned? Are there areas of deception that need the light of truth? Are you seeking—truly seeking—to please the Lord in the way you conduct your life? Is your home a place where you hate sin and want what honors the Lord?

The call of discipleship is a call to love—to love God and your neighbors. Jesus said others would recognize his disciples by their love for each other (John 13:35), and love is the first fruit of the Spirit that Paul lists (Gal. 5:22–23). The home of a disciple, then, is a crucial context where love for God and love for neighbors are lived out.

Living alone doesn't have to mean always being alone. Have you considered how a disciple's holy life will intersect with others through hospitality?

Your dining room table is a place for salt in more ways than one. Though Jesus's accusers despised his association with sinners, with his befriending words and welcoming presence, he treated others like people of worth, people made in God's image.

Building relationships also builds credibility. When we welcome people into our homes, they can experience hospitality as the warm and welcoming hand of Christ. The power of Christian love and hospitality is especially evident in a polarizing culture. With civil discourse descending lower and lower into tribalism, the alienation of our neighbors presents believers with a heavy opportunity and responsibility. In a culture full of hatred, Christian love is refreshing and surprising.

The Mystery of Marriage

Many of you reading these words are married. Your marriage in your home is to be a union that pictures the Christ-church covenant. In Genesis, the writer said a man will leave his father and mother and be united to his wife as one flesh (Gen. 2:24). This one-flesh union is part of God's epic story of redemption. The husband-wife relationship testifies to the greater and everlasting covenant between Christ and his bride, the church (Eph. 5:32).

If you are married, God has joined you together (Mark 10:9). And the gospel is good news for your home. Loving your spouse is part of your calling as a disciple of Christ. A marriage relationship must be characterized by virtues such as patience, forbearance, forgiveness, and self-control. A spouse is a sinner married to a sinner, and thus the challenge of loving another person occurs in the midst of human selfishness and inconsideration. We can harm others with our words and actions. We have the capacity to deeply wound a fellow image-bearer.

Scripture tells of God's enduring and steadfast love for his people. Though the Israelites were unfaithful, the Lord pursued them in love (Hosea 1:2; Ezek. 16:60–63). He would not repay their unfaithfulness with unfaithfulness. The use of marital language for God and his people indicates that the design of marriage points to truths beyond a mere human covenant (2 Cor. 11:2; Eph. 5:25).

The mystery of marriage is that it ultimately points to the covenant between Christ and his church (Eph. 5:32). This is the big picture, the revelation to which marriages throughout all human history point. While there have been billions of marriages, there has never been a relationship like that of Jesus and his bride. In fact, one way to tell God's story of salvation is with marriage language. The Bible begins and ends with a wedding. In the Garden of Eden, Adam and Eve were married, and at the end of Revelation, the New Jerusalem comes down from heaven like a bride beautifully prepared for her husband (Rev. 21:2).

If you are married, you are part of a good yet temporary union that will give way to an eternal reality. Earthly marriages are not meant to be eternal. There is no marriage in the age to come (Matt. 22:30). Jesus will forever be the bridegroom, and the church will forever be his bride. Earthly covenants end at death, so God's purposes will climax in the fullness of the heavenly covenant between God and his people. The joyful and eternal union of Jesus with his church is far superior to the happiest earthly marriage.

Four Reminders for Christian Marriage

It is easy to forget that we are part of a bigger picture. We can get caught up in the mundane details of life and lose perspective. By applying the gospel to our marriage, we will aim to avoid the pitfalls that derail marriages and send them down joyless paths.

First, all spouses are incompatible sinners. Apart from Christ, none of us are fundamentally compatible with anyone else. Our spouse's sin aggravates our sin. His anger makes her angry. Her condescension aggravates his pride. His selfishness makes her withdraw from intimacy. Her spitefulness tempts him to harbor bitterness. His laziness tries her impatience. Her free spending provokes his greed. It's sin against sin, sinner against sinner.

No spouse can meet your every need and fulfill your every longing. No one meets your every expectation, not even *you*. If you were married to yourself, you would be left unfulfilled and disappointed. You shouldn't treat your spouse like a functional god—as your anchor, your hope in this world, your unshakable rock, or your satisfaction. Don't look to your spouse for what you should seek in God alone. Storms are coming in your marriage. Where will you look for hope? Who will you trust when trust is broken in your marriage? What will you do when physical illness, emotional break-down, or spiritual depression comes? A marriage centered on the glory of God has a covenantal core that is stronger than any human sin threatening to tear it apart.

Second, God's plan for our holiness includes learning the sufficiency of his grace. Trying in our own strength to live as godly husbands and wives should reinforce our inability to meet God's standards. We are powerless to change others, and we are not able to bring godly change within ourselves. If marriage doesn't teach us to depend on God, we're not paying close enough attention to our sinfulness.

Paul learned that weakness was the platform for God's strength (2 Cor. 12:9–10). Do you trust God enough to believe your sufferings may be the Lord's way of keeping you from further sin (2 Cor. 12:7)? Christians need to preach to themselves the sanctifying power of the gospel for their marriages. On the cross, God's grace accomplished what our works never could—redemption. This same redeeming grace can teach two sinners how to glorify God in a marital covenant.

Third, the New Covenant shapes the marriage covenant. Paul has words for wives: "Wives, submit to your own husbands, as to the Lord. For the husband is the head of the wife even as Christ is the head of the church, his body, and is himself its Savior. Now as the church submits to Christ, so also wives should submit in everything to their husbands" (Eph. 5:22–24). And Paul has words for husbands: "Husbands, love your wives, as Christ loved the church and gave himself up for her, that he might sanctify her, having cleansed her by the washing of water with the word, so that he might present the church to himself in splendor, without spot or wrinkle or any such thing, that she might be holy and without blemish" (Eph. 5:25–27). Words like *Christ*, *church*, and *Savior* denote the New Covenant since Christ is the Savior of the church.

Two-headed creatures aren't natural, and neither is a two-headed marriage. The husband is the head of the marriage as Christ is the head of the church, and the wife is called to submit to her husband as the church does to Christ, but both spouses have the same spiritual status before God—justified by grace alone through faith alone. Roles of leadership and submission are not about inferiority or superiority. If wives neglect to reflect on the relationship between Christ and his bride, they will fall prey to the misunderstandings of the culture and distort biblical submission. The bride of Christ should gladly affirm and follow the authority of Christ, and likewise wives should gladly affirm and follow the leadership of their husbands. However, just as the bride of Christ should never engage in sin, wives should never follow their husband in disobedience to God. The husband's biblical headship means sacrifice (Eph. 5:25), holiness (Eph. 5:26–27), love (Eph. 5:25, 28), care (Eph. 5:29), and devotion (Eph. 5:31). Paul's language ran counter to his culture and ours. It is a Christian worldview that esteems wives as respectable and valuable people. Husbands and wives, you must preach to yourselves the gospel because it proclaims the sacrificial work of Christ that purchased the church. And his cross—an instrument of sacrifice and love—must be central to your marriage covenant.

Fourth, grace accomplishes what the law cannot. Grace brings transformation, while the law brings condemnation. In marriage, we must be people of grace or we are doomed to continually berate each other for unmet expectations. Law, not grace, comes naturally to us. We make demands of ourselves and others, wanting things to be done in certain ways. Forgetting (or ignoring) the fact that the law cannot accomplish what grace can, Christian spouses can live with unending frustration and anger. Through Christ we have been reconciled to God, and now we stand and live in grace (Rom. 5:2). The Christian life is all of grace. Since God sanctifies us with his redeeming grace, we cannot be indifferent to how we live as Christian spouses. We have been forgiven by Christ, and now marriage provides us with countless opportunities to show that grace to others. Paul Tripp wrote, "More couples than I can number have been surprised that their marriage needs the regular rescue of grace."[1]

To be gracious in marriage, we need the transforming power of the Spirit at work in us. Do you daily seek the Lord's redeeming grace to sanctify your heart and mind? Preaching God's grace to yourself will empower you to show grace to your spouse. As a Christian spouse, you need God's grace today, and you will need it tomorrow. Does the Lord's patience with you soften your heart toward your spouse? Does the Lord's forgiveness of your sins increase your compassion toward your spouse? Does the Lord's daily bestowal of grace on your life motivate you to show grace toward your spouse? Grace should beget more grace. The law kills whatever it touches. If Jesus bore the curse of the law in our place (Gal. 3:13), then don't lay the law on your spouse for whom Jesus also died. Law cannot bring transformation, but grace can.

The Weight of Parenting

The gospel that is for marriage is the same gospel that is for parents. We are parenting people who will stand before God. Does that end-time reality impact the way you think about your parenting responsibilities? We're parenting sinners. They may be cute sinners who do funny things, but they're also selfish. Children want their way. They lack wisdom and are bent toward foolishness.

For the challenging task of raising children, parents have the good news of Christ Jesus crucified and risen. We are representatives of the Lord. We are mouthpieces of rescuing grace. While Christian parents should want their children to change and grow in matters of obedience, this goal will never be accomplished by mere behavior modification. A deeper change is necessary, and all parents are helpless to bring about that transformation in the souls of their children. We can't threaten or bully them into the kingdom of Christ.

---

1. Paul David Tripp, *What Did You Expect? Redeeming the Realities of Marriage* (Wheaton, IL: Crossway Books, 2010), 20.

The great weight of parenting is felt at the intersection of what we want for our children's hearts and what our limits are. But because the Lord uses means to accomplish his ends, parents should submit to the wisdom of scripture with dependence and trust.

A Parent Who Walks with God

The most important thing your children need to see is your love for God lived out. The fear of the Lord must never remain an abstract concept we ascribe to. The fear of the Lord is the beginning of wisdom (Prov. 9:10), and to live wisely means to live skillfully before God and others. Our children need to see our reverence for God and our desire to honor God.

Example and exhortation go together. Paul said, "Fathers, do not provoke your children to anger, but bring them up in the discipline and instruction of the Lord" (Eph. 6:4). This calling fits with Proverbs where the son is called to hear his father's instruction and not forsake his mother's teaching (Prov. 1:8). Children can notice—with penetrating insight—if mom or dad is just going through spiritual motions but not actually loving Christ.

Since Christians are repenting sinners, Christian parents must be repenting sinners. Are there areas of disobedience you're indulging in, justifying, or ignoring? Do our children understand that we need the Lord's grace and that we don't have it all together? It is not weakness to admit your dependence on Christ. In the paradoxical design of Christ's kingdom, humility doesn't undermine authority but rather establishes it. Humility doesn't compromise your parental authority.

You will sin against your children. You will make false assumptions. You will render bad judgments. You will get plenty of things wrong, but God didn't set you in your home because he'd overlooked your inadequacies. Your weakness is the place for his strength. Parenting is not conditioned on whether you have it all together. Faithful parenting is consistently leading your children to understand God's provision of a rescuer in Jesus Christ. Don't hide the truth that you desperately need the Lord's grace. Your children need to know and see God's gracious rescue at work in your own life. They need to see someone who walks with God.

A Love That Perseveres

We're never fully prepared to be a parent, for we don't know the future and therefore can't fully anticipate what challenges are down the road. But as ambassadors of the Lord Jesus, Christian parents should help children glimpse the everlasting love of God through persevering love. Children will say and do things that wound and discourage us. But hasn't our offensiveness toward God been greater? Let us be awestruck that God's persevering love has endured our defiance, our rebellion, and our unbelief.

Does your love for your children seek peace and reconciliation? Does your love cover offenses and extend forgiveness? Does your love address disobedience in your children and apply discipline? One way to understand love is that someone acts for the good of another. Love is active and directional. The love we need for our children is a persevering love, and how wonderful to have the supreme example of God's persevering love that he demonstrated toward us in his Son. Paul says that nothing—neither death nor life, neither angels nor rulers, neither the present nor the future—can separate us from God's love (Rom. 8:38–39).

I wonder if your children sense security in your love or if they see your love as conditioned on their performance. Do you strive to parent with their greatest good in mind? What their hearts most need is not perfect grades, sports scholarships, popularity, social affirmation, or positions of power. Their greatest need corresponds to their greatest problem. Children have the intractable problem of sin, so they need a rescuer. And only the good news of Christ Jesus proclaims the rescuer for sinners of any age. Let us point them eagerly and urgently to the persevering love of God that took the shape of a rugged cross outside Jerusalem.

Children under Authority

Maybe you're reading this book and living at home under the authority of your parents. Paul's letters addressed children in the local churches because discipleship is not just for adults. If you're a young disciple of Christ, your home is a sphere where you work out your salvation with fear and trembling (Phil. 2:12–13).

Obedience to parents is part of obedience to the Lord. Paul wrote, "Children, obey your parents in the Lord, for this right" (Eph. 6:1). The fifth commandment is about honoring your father and mother (Exod. 20:12). To honor your parents is to esteem them in your heart. Honoring them is not merely outward conformity to the regulations in the home. The home is a crucial place for you to learn submission and deference to authority so you can operate wisely and honorably toward authorities outside your home.

Honoring your parents won't always mean agreeing with your parents. You may think they're underreacting to some things and overreacting to other things, and sometimes you may be right. But a joyful disposition of submission is a deep mark of God's grace in a child.

Growing Up and Growing Wiser

Scripture speaks to the young and issues a plea for right worship and obedience to God. The writer of Ecclesiastes says, "Remember also your Creator in the days of your youth" (Eccles. 12:1). And to the son in Proverbs, the father says, "Trust in the LORD with all your heart, and do not lean on your own understanding. In all your ways acknowledge him, and he will make straight your paths" (Prov. 3:5–6).

Wisdom is not just for the aged. We should walk wisely before God early in life. Don't conclude that your teenage years belong to you. Don't live like your 20s are your possession. All life and breath are from above. Rebellion is not a necessary stage for the young. Rebellion against God is dangerous and destructive. When God calls the young to embrace wisdom, he's intervening in foolishness by extending his rescuing grace. Wisdom leads away from the stupidity of sin. Wisdom brings order to the chaos that sin causes. Wisdom exposes the lies of temptation. How we need wisdom, then, and as soon as possible!

Early in life, let us establish the discipline of going to a Bible-loving church and connecting through membership and service. Even if you're the only one in your family who attends, you should go out of obedience to Christ and for the good of your soul. Maintain a discipline of daily Bible reading and prayer. Form friendships with others who love and follow Christ. Your close companions will either help you grow in wisdom or prove to be hindrances to holiness. Your peer group shouldn't be the decisive influence on you. In addition to church involvement, find an older and godly mentor who will pour into you and help you grow in your devotion to Christ.

Crucified in the Home

Whether you're single or married, a parent or a child, the good news is for you, and it needs to impact your home. Jerry Bridges wrote, "We are saved by grace, and we are to live by grace every day of our Christian lives."[2] The powerful gospel that saves us is the same gospel that sanctifies us. When we submit to Jesus as Savior and Lord, we are receiving life-giving news that has a depth and breadth we cannot fully fathom.

True Christians are Christ-centered people. Paul said that Jesus died for us "that those who live might no longer live for themselves but for him who for their sake died and was raised" (2 Cor. 5:15). Before coming to know Jesus, sinners lived for themselves. Self was king; self was god. But the path of self-exaltation is miserable and leads to judgment. We were not made for treasuring ourselves above all things. In the message of the gospel, we learn that Christ calls us away from the folly of self-worship and idolatry. Living for self is a tragic and God-dishonoring pursuit, a pursuit from which we need deliverance. Living for self is so Christ-belittling that Jesus died to deliver sinners from such a human-centered and condemnable existence. Now, instead of living for themselves, Christians must deny themselves, take up their cross, and follow Jesus (Luke 9:23). Jesus was raised to life so we might live a new life, a life centered on him.

As we awaken each day in our homes, ready to engage the responsibilities before us and the world around us, we need to ponder the new life we've been given in Christ. Paul said, "I have been crucified with Christ. It is no longer I who live, but Christ who lives in me. And the life I now live in the flesh I live by faith in the Son of God, who loved me and gave himself

2. Bridges, *The Discipline of Grace*, 19.

for me" (Gal. 2:20). Believers can say with Paul, "I have been crucified with Christ." Through faith we are united to Jesus and thus to his life.

In union with Jesus, we experience a death to sin and self. A decisive break has occurred from our human-centered, Christ-belittling ways. This decisive break is a *death*. "Do you not know that all of us who have been baptized into Christ Jesus were baptized into his death? We were buried therefore with him by baptism into death, in order that, just as Christ was raised from the dead by the glory of the Father, we too might walk in newness of life" (Rom. 6:3–4).

Alive now to God, we must reject the allure of self-exaltation as we follow Christ. In Luke 9:23, Jesus said that a disciple must take up his cross *daily*. The call to death is an invitation to greater life, true life. Dietrich Bonhoeffer wrote, "The cross is not the terrible end to an otherwise god-fearing and happy life, but it meets us at the beginning of our communion with Christ. When Christ calls a man, he bids him come and die."[3]

Conclusion

No matter your relationship status or home address, the good news is for you. Jesus calls us to follow him with our remaining breath. He becomes the reason for living and dying; he is not a means to some greater end. Christ is ultimate. Paul wrote that "to live is Christ, and to die is gain" (Phil. 1:21). If Paul lost everything, he would do so gladly so that Christ might be seen as more precious and worthy (Phil. 3:7–8). By the gracious work of the Spirit through faith in Christ, we are now alive to God for the glory of God. Sin is not the reigning power over us. God's grace has intervened when we were foolishly devoted to self and sin. The implications for our relationships are profound and ongoing. As our age increases and as stages in life change, let us trust the Lord's providence regarding where we are and who we're with. Let us labor for their soul's greatest good by pointing people to the world's greatest news.

---

3. Bonhoeffer, *The Cost of Discipleship*, 89.

10
A FUTURE FULL OF HOPE

Every generation of believers faces the challenge of grounding Christian growth and discipleship in the gospel. But the gospel must not be assumed. It must be taught, proclaimed, and defended. Pointing people to the gospel is no guarantee they will embrace it, but the results aren't in our hands. God builds his church, and the gates of hell cannot overcome it. The saints of God are walking step-by-step into a future full of hope.

Speaking of Greater Wonders

The Bible commands believers to pass on the faith to the next generation, so we cannot be silent (Deut. 6:4–7, 20–25; Ps. 147:4–7, 11–12). For others to embrace truth, we have to share it with them. For people to worship God, we need to tell about him and his mighty deeds. This calls for strategic speech. We cannot be thoughtless and incomplete about the faith; we must be thorough and intentional in communicating the content of the gospel.

To faithfully communicate the gospel, we first need to understand it ourselves. When the Old Testament authors called for people to impart the truths of God to the next generation, uppermost in their minds was his deliverance in the Exodus and the giving of his righteous laws from Sinai and the tabernacle. God revealed himself, and for future people to know the Lord, they needed to know and embrace his revelation.

The New Testament era was the time of fulfillment when the promises and hopes of the Old Testament came streaming together in the person and work of Jesus Christ. Better than the Exodus from Egypt, Jesus delivers from sin and hell. The wonders in the ministry of Jesus surpass the wonders in the Old Testament. Knowing this truth, how can we remain silent?

Words Necessary

God taught his people not only through *works* but through *words*. The psalmist said, "He established a testimony in Jacob and appointed a law in Israel, which he commanded our fathers to teach to their children, that the next generation might know them, the children yet unborn, and arise and tell them to their children, so that they should set their hope in God and not forget the works of God, but keep his commandments" (Ps. 78:5–7).

The people of Israel were responsible to pass on the word of God to their children for the sake of future generations. The focus in the psalmist's words is not the next generation but the ones beyond it. One way we care for the future and nourish hope in God's people is by clearly and faithfully proclaiming the gospel to those who are coming after us. The psalmist wants us to care about people not yet born. What we want are generations of worshipers who remember God and keep his commands in the power of the Spirit.

But can't our lives communicate the truth about Christ? What about the saying from Francis of Assisi: "Preach the gospel everywhere you go. And if necessary, use words"? Well, problem number one is that Francis of Assisi never said that. It's falsely attributed to him all the time. Second, the statement isn't biblical, regardless of who said it. The sentiment behind the saying is that we should live out what we believe, and to that we say yes and amen. But the gospel is *news*, and news must be shared, taught, explained, and passed on. You can't look at someone's life and arrive at a sound Christology. You can't look at someone's life and understand what happened on the cross.

Words are necessary to convey the gospel. If the next generation does not know the authoritative Word and powerful works of God, they will be stubborn and rebellious with disloyal hearts and ignorant minds. This is no empty warning. It's happened before.

Learning from Past Mistakes

Judges 2 describes what results when a generation fails to pass on the Word and wonders of God. When the generation of Joshua died, "there arose another generation after them who did not know the LORD or the work that he had done for Israel" (Judg. 2:10). Doesn't it grieve you to read this? Doesn't it seem nearly inconceivable that the descendants of the Exodus people—these sons and daughters of the wilderness who grew up on manna and watched the older generation die off under judgment while they wandered, these Israelites who had walked across the Jordan River and saw the walls of Jericho fall—didn't tell the ones after them about Yahweh?

In the next verse we're told that "the people of Israel did what was evil in the sight of the LORD and served the Baals" (Judg. 2:11). The Baals! The deeds of the Israelites were wicked, and their worship was false. The tragedy of Judges 2:11 is set in the context of 2:10. When the Israelites forsook the Lord, one reason was the neglect by previous generations to pass on the words and works of God. These people were ignorant of what God said and did because no one told them.

We must never assume the gospel. If we do not pass on the faith, once for all delivered to the saints, there will arise people who do not know the words and works of God.

Holding Firmly to the Word

We will not be able to pass on what we do not hold. Paul said, "Now I would remind you, brothers, of the gospel I preached to you, which you received, in which you stand, and by which you are being saved, if you hold fast to the word I preached to you—unless you believed in vain" (1 Cor. 15:1–2). The content of the gospel tradition comes next:

For I delivered to you as of first importance what I also received: that Christ died for our sins in accordance with the Scriptures, that he was buried, that he was raised on the third day in accordance with the Scriptures, and that he appeared to Cephas, then to the twelve. Then he appeared to more than five hundred brothers at one time, most of whom are still alive, though some have fallen asleep. Then he appeared to James, then to all the apostles. Last of all, as to one untimely born, he appeared also to me.

—1 Cor. 15:3–8

The logic unfolding in 1 Corinthians 15:1–8 goes like this: Paul received what was of "first importance," and he delivered it to the Corinthians who were receptive. The gospel Paul preached is the gospel the Corinthians received and by which they were being saved. If the professing Christians forsook the gospel, they would demonstrate vain belief that seemed to be real at first but proved otherwise.

Central to the gospel news is the death, burial, and resurrection of Jesus. This emphasis is not to minimize Jesus's miraculous conception or sinless life. Those truths are vital as well. In addition to this, the ascension and present reign of Christ are part of the gospel news. Paul's language in 1 Corinthians 15 points to the tradition about Christ's sin-bearing death and prophesied deliverance. Scripture's patterns and prophecies expected a suffering and vindicated redeemer.

What Paul gave to the Corinthians they were to pass onto others. The saints needed not only to know the gospel clearly but to hold to it firmly.

The Gospel Content

If the gospel were a box we opened, what would we find inside?

First, Jesus was miraculously conceived. He is truly divine and truly human, the God-man. This affirmation matters because if Jesus were only human, his death on the cross would do nothing to satisfy the justice of God for sinners. The virginal conception of Jesus is important to his identity. If the virginal conception of Jesus isn't true, then the rest of the good news doesn't matter. A Jesus who isn't divine is a Jesus who isn't a Savior of sinners.

Second, Jesus lived a sinless life. Never once did he sin, neither in conduct nor in his heart. He was born under the reign of the Mosaic Law, and

134

he fulfilled its statutes perfectly. The purity of Jesus is indispensable to the work of the cross. If Jesus ever sinned, he would need a savior. Only as a sinless person could he serve as the sacrificial substitute. He who knew no sin became the sin offering for us.

Third, Jesus laid down his life through death on a cross. His humble submission to suffering and crucifixion meant that his life would end. The cross became the place of the substitution, and Jesus was the offering. He died for our sins as he bore them, paying the price of sin's wages. Before his last breath, he said, "It is finished!" (John 19:30). There on the cross, a sufficient atoning sacrifice established a new covenant.

Fourth, Jesus was buried. The burial of Jesus confirms his death. During this time he was disembodied—soul separated from body. The presence of his body in the grave was a visible reminder that the cords of corruption would seize his remains and do what they had done to millions of bodies before him. Roman soldiers guarded the tomb to prevent anyone from violating the scene and stealing the body. The burial of Jesus had signaled his defeat.

Fifth, Jesus rose from the dead. The resurrection was the defeat of death. The glorified life of Christ launched the new creation of God in a fallen world. Death would not be an obstacle to Christ's everlasting rule and priesthood. The resurrection of Jesus is so vital to Christianity that Paul says our faith is futile without it. Through bodily resurrection, Jesus is the last Adam who is turning back the effects of the curse that came through the disobedience of the first Adam.

Sixth, Jesus ascended to the Father. The ascension confirms the present reign of Christ. All authority in heaven and on earth belongs to him. He is the reigning head of the church, his body. And in ascended majesty, Christ is the praise of heaven. He builds his church through the spread of the gospel, and he will subject all enemies under his feet. When the saints call Jesus the King of kings, they are declaring a truth that is not wholly future. Jesus is King now.

Seventh, Jesus will return. The risen Son is the judge of the earth. He will return to raise the dead, and before him the nations will gather.

The wicked will enter everlasting judgment while the righteous enter everlasting life. The return of Christ ensures the vanquishing of evil. No earthly leader and no amassing army will withstand the sovereign Lord. He will fully overcome the effects of sin and death in creation. That accomplishment will be a new creation where nothing unclean will dwell and where the people of God will live with their Creator and Redeemer in everlasting joy.

The people of God need the whole gospel. We have news that not only is Jesus redeeming sinners but he will also make all things new. If any of the previous seven gospel truths are rejected, the rest of the gospel crumbles.

Gospel Awakening

Because the gospel is the power of God, we can be confident in hearts waking up to its glory. Let's drive our ministries with the gospel. Let's center our homes on the gospel. Let's root our lives in the gospel. What is there to fear? Believers have proclaimed the good news of Christ Jesus for 2,000 years, and the message has not lost one ounce of power.

It is thrilling to hear stories of people waking up to the depth and splendor of who Jesus is and what he accomplished. This waking up is vital for holding firm. When we see—truly behold—the truth of Christ in scripture, we will not want to minimize or sideline it in search of deeper, more profound ideas. We will see clearly that nothing is more profound than the love of God demonstrated in sending his Son for sinners.

Part of how gospel awakening happens is by preaching Jesus from the Old Testament. There were years in my preaching ministry when I emphasized the New Testament to the neglect of the Old Testament. I needed to realize afresh that the Old Testament is Christian scripture, and I needed that truth to impact my preaching. Do you believe that Jesus is the point of the Old Testament? Paul said, "All Scripture is breathed out by God and profitable for teaching, for reproof, for correction, and for training in righteousness, that the man of God may be complete, equipped for every good work" (2 Tim. 3:16–17).

When we proclaim the riches of the gospel from Genesis to Revelation, the eyes and ears of the listeners will encounter the single story of God's redemptive plan. And this plan is thrilling to understand. Gospel awakening will come through gospel preaching, and this preaching must include the whole counsel of scripture. Jesus is the seed of the woman in Genesis 3, he is the final Passover Lamb in Exodus 12, he is the sacrifice of atonement in Leviticus 16, he is the object raised to save the perishing in Numbers 21, he is the prophet like Moses in Deuteronomy 18, and we could go on and on. When we go into Old Testament scripture to read it in light of Christ's person and work, those 39 books open riches and glories we will marvel at for the rest of our lives.

Dark Valleys Ahead

Since we walk by faith and not by sight, Christ must be our confidence. His power prevails over the darkness, so a gospel boldness is necessary for dark seasons ahead. We don't know the suffering that awaits us. We don't know the obstacles our local churches will face. We don't know what prowling plans the devil has for the global church.

But we do know that the gospel is light in the darkness because it proclaims the light of the world. There's nothing like persecution to reveal the impotence of pragmatism. What is the hope for the underground churches in countries hostile to Christians? What is the hope for the unreached tribes and communities? The gospel is the certain power of our faithful God. Our hope is in what he has revealed through his Son. We can walk through dark valleys knowing that through many tribulations we will enter the kingdom (Acts 14:22). But the gospel will not fail because God cannot fail.

One reason Christians need the gospel is because all our days are uncertain. If our hope is in the comforts found in this world, what will become of our devotion to Christ when those comforts are lost? If our hope is in the success of our plans working out the way we think they should, what will become of our devotion to Christ when our plans collapse under the burdens of life and the inevitability of tragedy?

Suffering may reveal that our hope hasn't been in Christ. Dark valleys can clarify what truths we believe and the foundation on which we've built our lives. The good news of Christ Jesus is that this broken world has an appointed consummation, a redemption. If people profess to know Christ but aren't holding to the gospel, they've abandoned the good news for something that isn't good.

Your Future Life

The gospel is the curriculum of discipleship. When Christians hold to the gospel, they can take heart that Christ has overcome the world. He has taken their sin onto himself. The worst that could happen to you has happened to Christ. He was condemned in your place. And now your future is eternal life. Your tribulations are accumulating to display a glory that outweighs them all.

Now, in our fumbling and frail way, we are following the Savior who will not fail us. He is before us and with us, in us and over us. Have you considered that every principality and power will bend the knee? The gospel proclaims that Jesus is Lord. And in union with Christ the Lord, we are not condemned. What about our past? We were crucified with Christ. We have died to sin. What about our present? We have been brought to new life in him. The life we live is by faith in the Son of God who loved us and died in our stead. What about our future? Christ and all that he has will be our inheritance. Everlasting life and glory will be our daily portion.

Conclusion

Believers should want the next generation to know and love the gospel. This goal requires speaking and teaching. It requires explaining and repeating. It requires prayerful dependence that God will do a work within the hearts of readers and hearers. When God's people treasure the gospel, they will find the fullness of God's Word unfolding for them with fresh delight because the redemptive plan centered on Christ Jesus has been the point of scripture from its opening verse. In the last book of the story, John tells us what the countless multitudes are crying out: "Salvation belongs to our God who sits on the throne, and to the Lamb!" (Rev. 7:10). That claim will always be true. No charge against God's people will succeed, and the saints will sing of the Lamb's victory. The gospel is for Christians, and the gospel is forever.

ACKNOWLEDGMENTS

I am grateful to Lucid Books for supporting a second edition of *The Gospel Is for Christians*. It has been a pleasure to work with them along the way.

I thank God for my parents who have always supported my commitment to ministry, no matter where it has led me.

The Lord has blessed me with three churches that have been places of affirmation and encouragement. The first was Baptist Temple Church in Edna, Texas, the church where I grew up and where I preached my first sermon in 1999. The second was First Baptist Church in Santo, Texas, where I had my first pastorate. I am forever grateful to God for my years of ministry there and for the great joy that characterizes my memories of the people there. The third is Kosmosdale Baptist Church in Louisville, Kentucky, where I now serve as pastor. What a blessing it is to enjoy their fellowship, to see their growth in the Lord, and to proclaim to them the riches of the Word.

I am deeply grateful to God for Stacie, my extraordinary wife and best friend. She carved out time to comb through the revision of this book. Her suggestions and encouragements were invaluable, and her wise influence is on each page.

BIBLIOGRAPHY

Bonhoeffer, Dietrich. *The Cost of Discipleship*. New York: Touchstone, 1959.

Bridges, Jerry. *The Discipline of Grace: God's Role and Our Role in the Pursuit of Holiness*. Colorado Springs, CO: NavPress, 1994.

Carson, D. A. *The Difficult Doctrine of the Love of God*. Wheaton, IL: Crossway Books, 2000.

Dever, Mark, and Paul Alexander. *The Deliberate Church: Building Your Ministry on the Gospel*. Wheaton, IL: Crossway Books, 2005.

DeYoung, Kevin, and Ted Kluck. *Why We Love the Church: In Praise of Institutions and Organized Religion*. Chicago: Moody Publishers, 2009.

Gilbert, Greg. *What Is the Gospel?* Wheaton, IL: Crossway, 2010.

Horton, Michael. *The Gospel-Driven Life: Being Good News People in a Bad News World*. Grand Rapids, MI: Baker Books, 2009.

Lewis, C. S. *Mere Christianity*. New York: Touchstone, 1952.

————. *Reflections on the Psalms*. New York: Harcourt Brace, 1958.

Lloyd-Jones, Martyn Dr. *Spiritual Depression: Its Causes and Its Cure*. Grand Rapids, MI: Wm. B. Eerdmans Publishing Co., 1965.

Packer, J. I. *Evangelism and the Sovereignty of God*. Downers Grove, IL: IVP Books, 1961.

————. *Knowing God*. Downers Grove, IL: InterVarsity Press, 1973.

Packer, J. I., and Mark Dever. *In My Place Condemned He Stood: Celebrating the Glory of the Atonement*. Wheaton, IL: Crossway Books, 2007.

Peterson, Eugene H. *A Long Obedience in the Same Direction: Discipleship in an Instant Society*. 2nd edition. Downers Grove, IL: IVP Books, 2000.

Piper, John. *Desiring God: Meditations of a Christian Hedonist*. Rev. ed. Colorado Springs, CO: Multnomah Publishers, 2003.

————. *God Is the Gospel: Meditations on God's Love as the Gift of Himself*. Wheaton, IL: Crossway Books, 2005.

————. *Let the Nations Be Glad! The Supremacy of God in Missions*. Rev. Ed. Grand Rapids, MI: Baker Academic, 2003.

————. *Spectacular Sins: And Their Global Purpose in the Glory of Christ*. Wheaton, IL: Crossway Books, 2008.

————. *When I Don't Desire God: How to Fight for Joy*. Wheaton, IL: Crossway Books, 2004.

Platt, David. *Radical: Taking Back Your Faith from the American Dream*. Colorado Springs, CO: Multnomah Books, 2010.

Spafford, Horatio. "It Is Well with My Soul" in "The American Colony in Jerusalem: A Family Tragedy." *Library of Congress*. https://www.loc.gov/exhibits/americancolony/amcolony-family.html.

Sproul, R. C. *The Holiness of God*. 2nd edition. Wheaton, IL: Tyndale House, 1998.

Spurgeon, Charles H. *The Complete Works of C. H. Spurgeon, Volume 60: Sermons 3387 to 3439*. Delmarva Publications, 2013. Google Books.

Tripp, Paul David. *What Did You Expect? Redeeming the Realities of Marriage*. Wheaton, IL: Crossway Books, 2010.

Wells, Paul. *Cross Words: The Biblical Doctrine of the Atonement*. Scotland: Christian Focus Publications, 2006.

CPSIA information can be obtained
at www.ICGtesting.com
Printed in the USA
BVHW040241240820
587115BV00004B/184